Acanthus
Carving
and Design

Bob Yorburg
Illustrations by Hans Sandom

4880 Lower Valley Road, Atglen, Pennsylvania 19310

Dedication

We would like to thank our wives and parents
for their continued support in this project and in life.

Other Schiffer Books on Related Subjects:
Chip Carving Nature: An Artistic Approach. Craig Vandall Stevens.
  ISBN: 0764300296. $12.95

Copyright © 2010 by Bob Yorburg
Illustration Copyright © 2010 by Hans Sandom

Library of Congress Control Number: 2010923804

All rights reserved. No part of this work may be reproduced
or used in any form or by any means—graphic, electronic, or
mechanical, including photocopying or information storage
and retrieval systems—without written permission from the
publisher.
The scanning, uploading and distribution of this book or any
part thereof via the Internet or via any other means without the
permission of the publisher is illegal and punishable by law. Please
purchase only authorized editions and do not participate in or
encourage the electronic piracy of copyrighted materials.
"Schiffer," "Schiffer Publishing Ltd. & Design," and the
"Design of pen and inkwell" are registered trademarks of Schiffer
Publishing Ltd.

Designed by Mark David Bowyer
Type set in University Roman Bd BT / New Baskerville BT

ISBN: 978-0-7643-3506-8
Printed in China

Schiffer Books are available at special discounts for bulk purchases
for sales promotions or premiums. Special editions, including
personalized covers, corporate imprints, and excerpts can be
created in large quantities for special needs. For more information
contact the publisher:

Published by Schiffer Publishing Ltd.
4880 Lower Valley Road
Atglen, PA 19310
Phone: (610) 593-1777; Fax: (610) 593-2002
E-mail: Info@schifferbooks.com

For the largest selection of fine reference books on this and
related subjects, please visit our web site at
www.schifferbooks.com
We are always looking for people to write books on new and
related subjects. If you have an idea for a book
please contact us at the above address.

This book may be purchased from the publisher.
Include $5.00 for shipping.
Please try your bookstore first.
You may write for a free catalog.

In Europe, Schiffer books are distributed by
Bushwood Books
6 Marksbury Ave.
Kew Gardens
Surrey TW9 4JF England
Phone: 44 (0) 20 8392 8585; Fax: 44 (0) 20 8392 9876
E-mail: info@bushwoodbooks.co.uk
Website: www.bushwoodbooks.co.uk

Contents

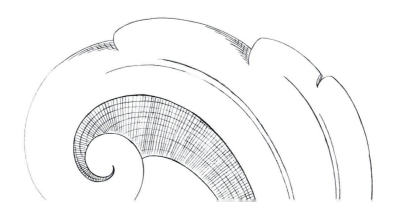

Acknowledgments

We would like to thank the following people for their diligent review of our many versions of this book and for their continued encouragement and prompting:

Laura Yorburg
Kathy Sandom
Betty Yorburg
Pam Hessey
Ken Defren
Peter Schiffer Sr.
Stefanie Rennert
Laurie Mann
Sara Durkacs
Jeff Snyder

To the Institute of Classical Architecture & Classical America we extend a heart felt thanks for allowing us to photograph and include pictures of its historical plaster cast collection donated to them by the Metropolitan Museum of Art.

We especially thank Pam Hessey for her guidance and input on the finishing chapter as well as the use of many spectacular photographs of her work.

There are many students, teachers, friends, and cohorts who have been instrumental in providing input and direction. We thank all of them as well.

Special thanks to Laura Yorburg, who contributed much and skillfully edited the manuscript.

Bob Yorburg
Hans Sandom

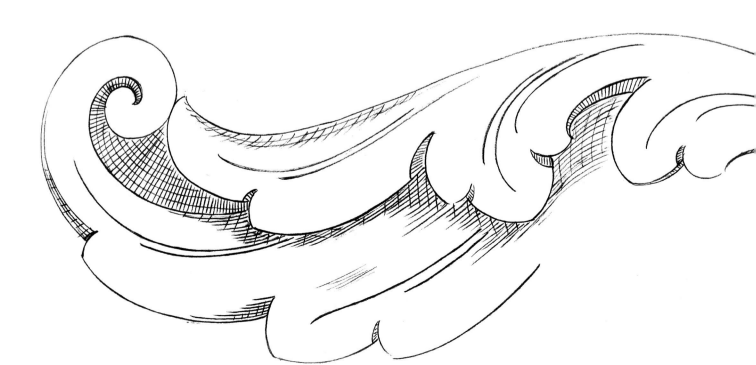

Preface

It is astounding that the acanthus motif as an ornament has been around for thousands of years, yet there is no source of design or declared technique in creating it. Myth tells us that this plant grew up around a column in ancient Greece. The builders and designers liked it so much that it became the capital ornament for Corinthian columns. From there the design spread like wildfire to Rome and ultimately to the rest of Europe. It is fascinating to see how the design has evolved and been interpreted in different countries. As time passed, the acanthus leaf motif spread through the realms of architecture, decorative items, furniture, marine carvings, signs, frames, and the printed page. Here is a decorative element that is ubiquitous, yet up until now no one has bothered to describe the process for creating it. This book is useful as both a guide in creating designs incorporating acanthus and a font of historical details and photographs. Through exposure to these elements, it is possible to gain a new appreciation of the world of design that surrounds us.

Note: Hand tools and power tools can be dangerous and must be used responsibly. Take all safety precautions including wearing goggles, hearing protection, and dust masks. Follow all manufacturers' recommendations. This book is a guide only. The authors and publisher of this book assume no responsibility for any injuries that may occur as a result of any readers' actions.

Chapter 1
Acanthus History and Lore

The Origin of a Style

Examples of acanthus design abound, yet few people know what acanthus is. Those "scrolly" leaves seen in architecture, furniture, fabric, frames, and more have become so stylized that the origin is often forgotten.

1.1 What is Acanthus?

The acanthus plant is a flowering, spiny-leaf plant native to the Mediterranean region (the southern parts of Europe and the warmer parts of Asia and Africa). The prefix of the Latin form of the Greek *akanthos* means "thorny," "a sharp point," a fair representation of the acanthus leaf. The modern common name for acanthus is bear's breech, formerly known as brank-ursine, which translates from *branca* (claw) + *ursinus*, belonging to a bear. The plant was so named because the leaf resembled a bear's claw. The two varieties that most influenced ancient Greek and Roman sculpture were the *Acanthus spinosus* and the *Acanthus mollis*. In the 1867 publication, *A Dictionary of Science and Art*, a key distinction is made about which species is used and where: "...but there is a difference between the Greek and Roman leaf; the former uses the *Acanthus spinosus*, or prickly acanthus; the latter the *Acanthus mollis*, the brank-ursine...". Whether or not this is true, the differences between the two varieties have little to do with interpretation in design.

No one really knows how the acanthus plant became such a prominent feature in ancient design. A persistent myth has it that in Corinth in the fifth century A.D. a prominent virgin died and was buried under a pyramidal tomb. Her loyal nurse or companion subsequently brought a chest to the gravesite, filled with the deceased's favorite jewels. In order to keep the air out and therefore keep the jewels preserved, she placed a tile over the chest. Unknowingly, this tribute was placed upon the root of an acanthus plant. As the plant sprung up, it grew haphazardly over the chest and up around the tile, its leaves taking on odd and beautiful shapes. Coincidentally, Callimachus, a celebrated sculptor of the time known for his delicate work in marble, sauntered by, noticed the beauty of nature's happenstance, and sketched the scene. The story ends with Callimachus borrowing nature's design to form one of his own, creating the Corinthian column. Myth or not, this is often how a work of art finds its beginnings and the story certainly provides undeniable romance.

On the other hand, the fifteenth century scholar and devout Jesuit, John Baptist Villalpando, alleged that the Corinthians copied the design from the Temple of Solomon, which was designed by none other than God himself. Furthermore, he stated that the columns were not crowned with acanthus at all, but rather palm branches, and that acanthus was rarely used by the Greeks. Renowned Viennese art historian Alois Riegla, (1858 – 1905) agreed. He argued that the leafy Greek ornamentation began as a sculptural version of the palmette and slowly developed into a resemblance of the acanthus.

These prominent historians seem to have been mistaken, since mention of acanthus exists in writings from the ancients themselves. The eminent Greek poet Ovid mentions acanthus being used as decoration during his period, 43 B.C. – A.D. 17 or 18. He describes an immense bronze vase with a border covered in acanthus. Another member of ancient Greek society was Athenaeus, a grammarian, rhetorician, and "banquet authority" who lived at the end of the second and beginning of the third centuries A.D. In one of his precious writings, he depicted the car in which Alexander the Great was transported to Egypt. He stated that the canopy was supported by golden columns intertwined with decorative acanthus.

1.2. Where to Find the Design

The acanthus plant has played an exceedingly important role in the history of art, decoration, and craftsmanship. From ancient Greece and Rome, the design traveled throughout the world and can be seen in everything from palaces to folk art. It appears in a variety of mediums including stone, metal, weaving, and painting; as well as in our own subject, acanthus carving and design.

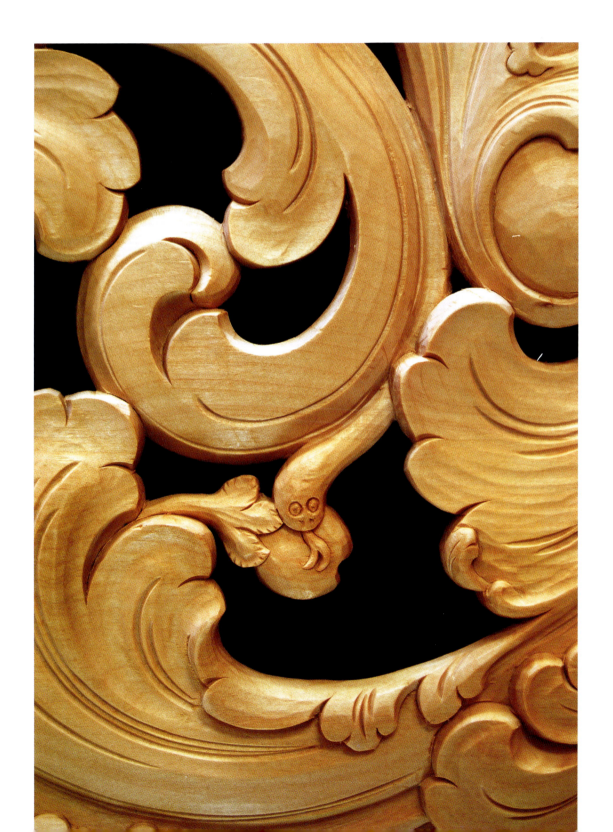

Chapter 2
Design

Good Carving
Begins with Good Design

2.1. How to Draw Patterns

A proper pattern yields beautiful flowing curves. It is amazing to see the number of historical carvings that were poorly executed. The eye often corrects the improper lines and the piece still evokes a pleasing sense. Here we will learn the basic techniques and elements involved in creating a design that includes the acanthus style. Where these elements are incorporated is entirely up to you. You might include them in printed material or a beautiful sign, frame or piece of furniture.

Let us begin with the form of the leaf itself. Acanthus leaves have many little spiny projections (Figure 2.1).

These projections have become stylized throughout the years and appear as ears or leaves off of the main scroll (Figure 2.2).

Figure. 2.2. Acanthus with ears or leaves

Figure 2.1. Acanthus Leaf

The scrolls themselves either exist as a C-scroll, an S-scroll or as a spiral. By combining these elements, a complete design can be created (Figures 2.3-2.5).

Figure 2.3. Example of a C-scroll

Figure 2.4. Example of an S-scroll

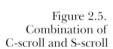

Figure 2.5. Combination of C-scroll and S-scroll

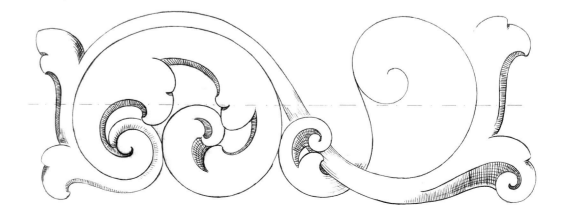

The Rococo and the Baroque styles feature C-scrolls & S-scrolls combined with shells, figures, floral, and fruit motifs. In joining the features in the Baroque style (Figure 2.6), there is a continuous flow, whereas the Rococo style (Figure 2.7) features elements that abut each other.

Figure 2.6. Example of Baroque style

Figure 2.7. Example of Rococo style

In the acanthus style, typically, every leaf in the design is traceable back to the root. This root serves to anchor the eye and provide a visual starting point for viewing the piece. The flow from there should be pleasing, graceful, and continuous. Choppy, uneven lines do not provide a nice basis for the design or carving (Figure 2.8).

Lines within the design must be continuous and each of the scroll portions should point to each other so that the entire scroll appears continuous (Figure 2.9a). If the edge of a scroll points off into outer space it looks very amateurish (Figure 2.9b)

Figure 2.9a. Correct

Figure 2.8. Drawing with choppy lines

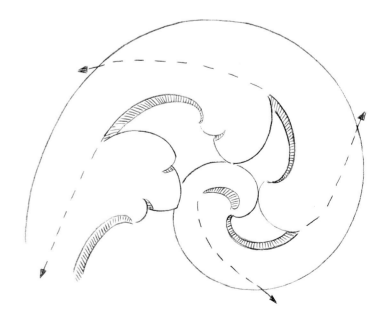

Figure 2.9b. Wrong

Now that you know the elements that make up the acanthus design, you must incorporate them into an overall context.

2.2. How to Lay Out Patterns

Generally, one should find a location that is appropriate to be enhanced with the acanthus motif. Once established, the overall shape and dimensions can be determined.

You can then fit the design to the space and shape it accordingly. Be certain that the lines flow. A good way to do this is not with a compass or "French Curve" but free hand. You can rest your wrist or arm on the table and describe an arc.

Interestingly, these lines are NOT parts of circles, but parts of spirals. The line is like a bent fishing pole. The beginning of the line is almost straight and the curve gets more pronounced as you travel along the curve. This is called an accelerated curve (Figure 2.10a); contrast this with a curved line (Figure 2.10b).

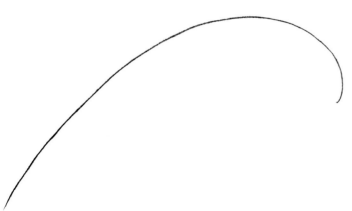

Figure 2.10a. Accelerated curve-line with tension

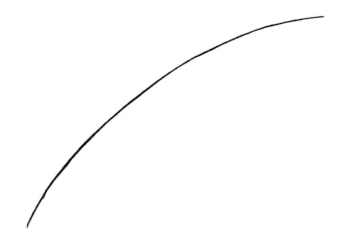

Figure 2.10b. Curved line with no tension

The accelerated curve creates much more interest and results in a very dynamic carving.

Be free handed when drawing the scrolls and leaves. With practice, the design will flow from your fingertips. Use the examples in this book as study guides, or you can order drawings from: **www.acanthuscarving.com**. Trace them over and over, and then try reproducing them freehand. Once you are familiar with the feel of this technique, you will be able to sketch the elements into many projects.

2.3. How to Transfer Patterns

This is where the fun begins. There are numerous ways to transfer patterns. The quick, old-fashioned way is to lay the pattern on the wood and trace the pattern with a piece of carbon paper below. Here are a few pointers to improve the process. Use graphite paper instead of carbon paper because it does not leave a greasy film that creates smudges. Also secure the edges of the pattern with repositionable tape or pins. The blue painter's masking tape is always good. The reason you want tape that is reusable is that you want to check the pattern to be assured that all of the elements have been transferred. Before removing the tape, it is helpful to draw a line from the edge of the pattern onto the wood in several places. These marks will serve as registration marks to realign the pattern on the wood should it be necessary to retrace any parts of the pattern later.

Another wonderful trick to transfer the pattern to the wood is to trace the lines with an empty ball point pen. The graphite paper beneath the pattern will transfer the design and the original pattern will remain unmarked. The pen is very precise and will not tear the original pattern. Be careful not to press too hard because you can leave impressions on the surface of the wood.

Reversing drawings is often necessary if the drawing is symmetrical. There are several ways to do this. One way is to put the original on a light box or window and trace the reversed image. Another way is to trace the original pattern with carbon or graphite paper below it facing up. The mirror image will be on the underside of the original pattern. You can also draw the pattern onto tracing paper with a pencil. Turn the pattern over onto a piece of wood and trace the pattern again with a pencil. The carbon on the underside of the tracing paper will appear on the wood. A quick way is to copy the pattern onto acetate in a copying machine and flip the acetate over. You have now created both sides of a symmetrical drawing. You may also scan the original image and reverse it in the computer with any number of programs. Please align the new pattern with the original and hold them up to the light. It is important to identify any distortions and correct them at this point.

For larger patterns, it is also possible to project an image via a slide projector, opaque projector or computer. Trace the pattern and correct the distortions. The pattern is then transferred to the wood.

Once the pattern is on the wood it is imperative to correct and improve the tracing before proceeding with carving. Often your tracing implement will tend to follow the grain rather than the pattern. Your crisp, flowing lines are often altered. It is best to stand back and visually inspect the drawing on the wood. Any place that appears choppy or a curve that is wavy needs to be gone over at this point. The best way to do this is with a dull pencil. A sharp pencil tends to get caught in the grain.

2.4. Enlarge, Reduce, & Adapt Designs

The oldest method for enlarging or reducing a pattern is to draw boxes over the original pattern. The resultant picture should look like the original with an overlay of a graph paper grid. Then decide how much you want the original enlarged or reduced. For example, if the new pattern is to be twice the size of the original, then draw the new grid twice the size of the original grid. Look at each of the original boxes and fill in the portion of the pattern in the larger box just the way it appears in the smaller box (Figures 2.11a & 2.11b). You will be surprised at how well this method works. Of course you will have to go over the entire drawing to clean it up.

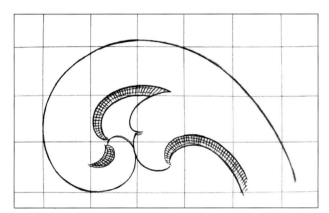

Figure 2.11a. Original

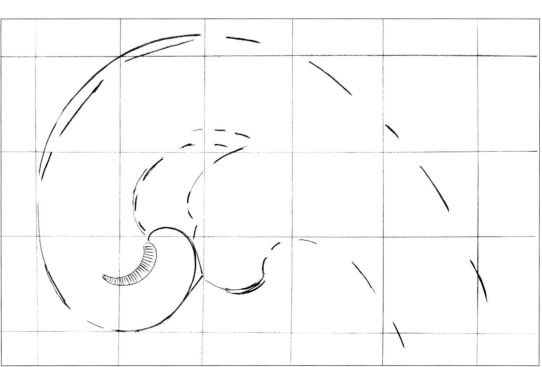

Figure 2.11b. Enlarged Version

Patterns may also be enlarged and reduced via copiers, projectors, and computers. Once the pattern is adjusted to the space available, it is often necessary to adapt the drawing to fit an unusual space or design. Architectural carvings must often fit into specific spaces. The approach is simple: add elements to fill in blank areas, but do not make the pattern too dense. Once again, stand back and review the design. You will be immediately aware of places that need to be corrected.

Here is the interesting part. Even though a pattern may look perfect in its flat state, it will definitely change once translated into a three-dimensional form. Therefore a pattern is only a guideline. Once you start carving, you might sketch it again many times as you progress with the carving. Another trick that works quite well is to use sign painter's application tape. This is a very thin translucent tape with low tack. It looks very much like masking tape. When laying out banners or scrolls on undulating surfaces, it is often necessary to have the pattern conform to the shape of the carving. A good example of this is the early American Bellamy style eagle (Figure 2.12). It is a very popular motif that most people have seen, possibly without knowing it. The banners blowing in the breeze often have lettering and acanthus details undulating with the piece. The effect is very pleasing and can only be successfully accomplished by drawing directly on the carving or on an overlay. The tape is nice because you can carve right through it and then peel it off. This leaves the carving clean. Another method is to spray the back of a copy of the pattern with removable spray adhesive. Apply this to the carving and start carving. It is generally best to sketch directly on the carving, but these other methods often save time and give extraordinary results.

Figure 2.12. Bellamy Eagle

2.5. How Angle of View Affects Design

This is an area that is often ignored in carving literature. You must take into account where the carving will live. For example, if the carving is to be up high, it (or part of it) should tilt down so that it may be seen more readily. If you are to examine the carvings of Tilmann Riemenschneider, (a carver from the fifteenth - sixteenth centuries) at eye level, the legs of people often appear too long. This is because many of his carvings were to occupy niches up high in churches. When looking up at the carvings, the eye foreshortens the lower part of the carving, or the legs, and everything looks exactly right. If you were to scale the figure off of a proportion wheel it would look as if the old masters had it all wrong. Instead, even 500 years ago, they were aware of the effect the viewing angle had on the finished product.

There is another reason to bear in mind the placement of the carvings in planning the execution of the finished product. That is time. Recently, there was an interesting exhibition at the Victoria and Albert Museum in London, England. On display was a series of carvings by Grinling Gibbons, known as the "King's Carver" in England (1648-1721). These carvings were removed after a fire and restored. Before being reinstalled in the various palaces, they were mounted on clear plastic and displayed to the public. What was most fascinating is that Mr. Gibbons was acutely aware of the placement of the carvings. Super detail was employed at eye level on the front of the carving. The detail rapidly fell off as the carving turned a corner and was only partially in view. The detail also decreased as the carvings were further away from the viewer. Additionally, the portions of the carvings that were barely seen or not seen at all were only rough carved. As such, you can imagine that an enormous amount of time was saved by not carving areas that were known to be unseen. Many small carvings are detailed throughout, yet if they are to reside in an alcove or high on a shelf, then the execution, details, and even proportions may want to be reconsidered.

2.6. Drawing Leaf Types and Scrolls

The following illustrations are examples of the types of leaves and effects that make up the overall design. Notice the shape of the design and the overall effect. All of the lines and planes in the entire baroque carving are contiguous and emanate from the root. The result will be of flowing, smooth lines resulting in a soothing effect. Any jarring angles or lines are assiduously avoided.

Single Leaf

In drawing a single leaf, you want to create a curve to denote motion and three-dimensionality. In Figure 2.13, the leaf might appear to bend to the right and/or arch up in the center. The leaf tip should never be skinny and pointy.

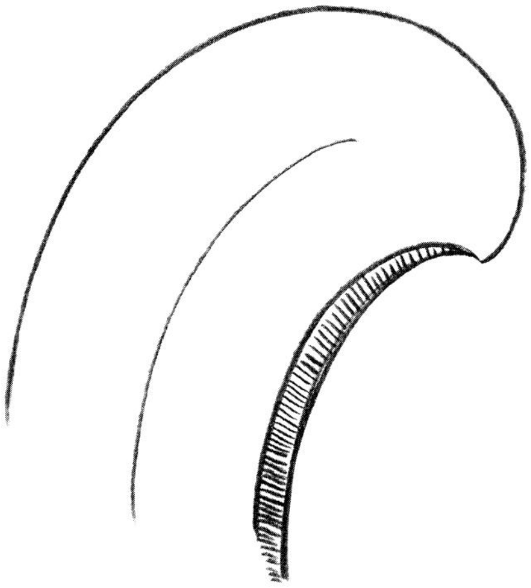

Double Leaf

In Figure 2.14a, notice that the lines start parallel at the base of the leaf and then splay apart. In Figure 2.14b, the small lobe is behind the tip and is situated approximately perpendicular to the axis of flow. Figure 2.14c shows the finished leaf with "veins" or "*geiss fuss*" lines drawn in. *Geiss fuss* is German for "goat's foot." These lines look similar to the marks that a goat with cloven hooves makes in the dirt, hence the expression, "*geiss fuss* lines." Figure 2.15 shows a double leaf with the lobe on the outside of the curve rather than the inside.

Figure 2.13. Single leaf

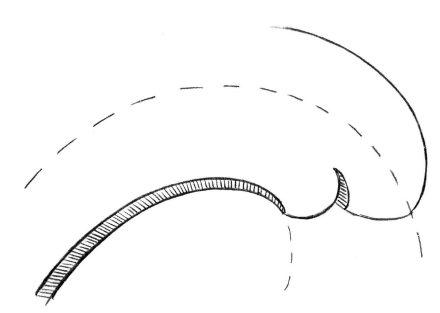

Figure 2.14a. Double
leaf shape

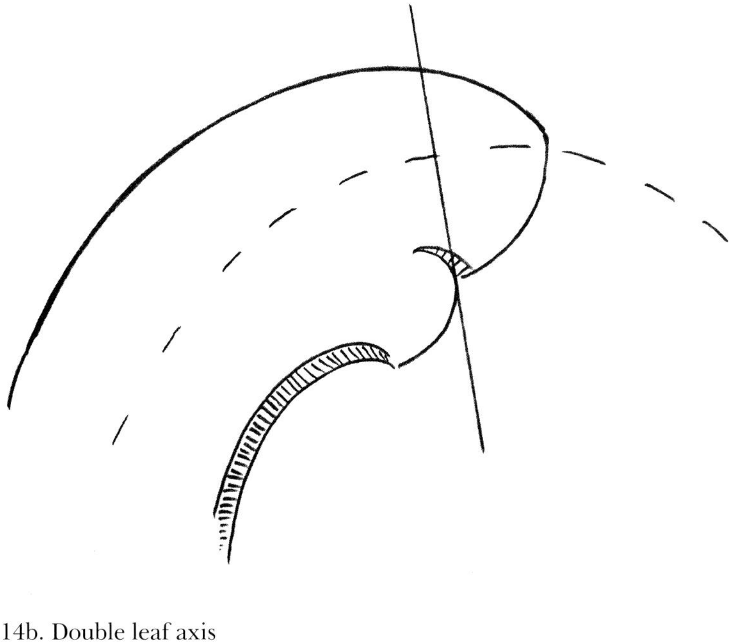

Figure 2.14b. Double leaf axis

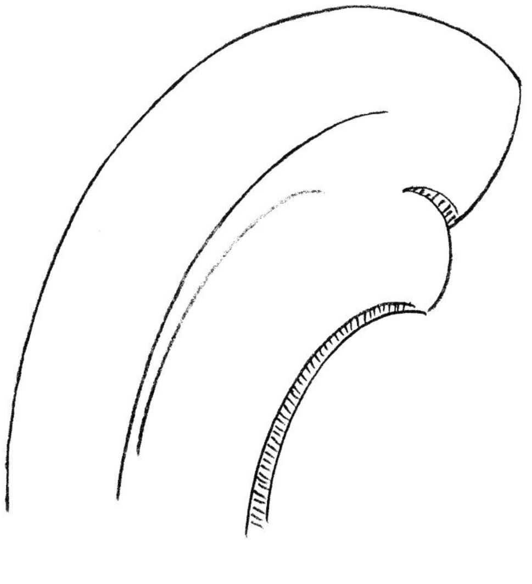

Figure 2.14c. Double leaf finished

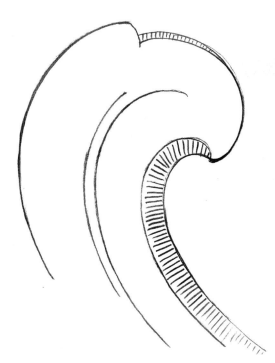

Figure 2.15. Double leaf with small lobe on the outside of the curve

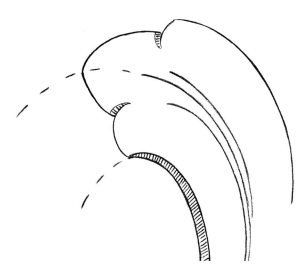

Figure 2.16b. Triple leaf correct

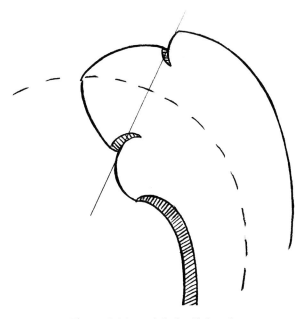

Figure 2.16c. Triple leaf lobe placement

Triple Leaf

Figure 2.16a shows the wrong way to draw a triple leaf. Notice that one of the axis lines shoots off into space. Figure 2.16b shows the correct way to draw a triple leaf. The axes begin virtually parallel and gracefully splay as they progress to the leaf tips. Figure 2.16c depicts lobe placement. Notice that the lobes illustrate a perpendicular line to the main axis. The smaller lobe always trails behind the larger lobe. Figure 2.16d represents the finished triple lobed leaf with the veins drawn in. Figure 2.17 illustrates how to carve the planes on a triple leaf. Take note that each of the planes is distinct and that they always follow the flow of the leaf.

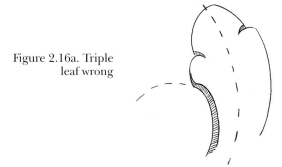

Figure 2.16a. Triple leaf wrong

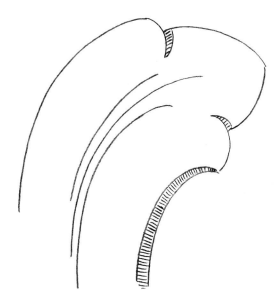

Figure 2.16d. Triple leaf finished

Combination Leaf

In Figure 2.18, you may view this as a leaf with a pair of two-lobed leaves. By shifting the position of the lobes, different effects can be established.

Leaf Ends

In Figure 2.19 you will notice that the end of the leaf still has the leaf tip curled in. This creates an "eye" that looks as though the leaf has not yet fully matured.

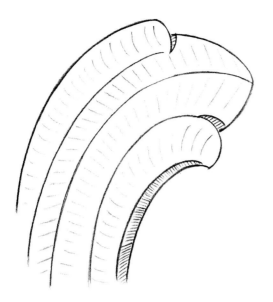

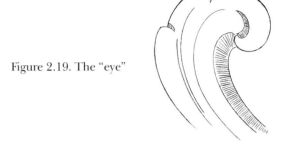

Figure 2.19. The "eye"

Figure 2.17. Triple leaf planes

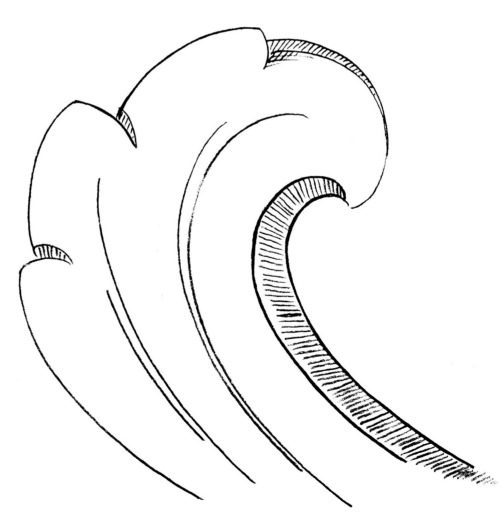

Figure 2.18. Combination of two double lobed leaves

The end of this leaf has not yet unfolded and it looks like a scroll (Figure 2.19a). The visual effect is different from the eye. Another version, shown in Figure 2.19b, shows how the tightness of the curve of the leaf effects the overall feeling evoked.

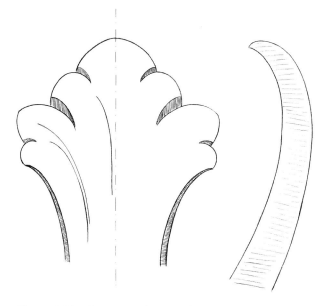

Figure 2.20. The crown, front and side views

Figure 2.19a. Leaf end with scroll

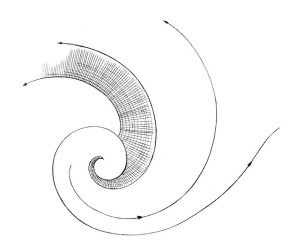

Figure 2.21a. The root

Figure 2.19b. Scroll end leaf with longer tip

The Crown

The crown can be made in many ways; basically it is a combination of leaf types. In the example shown in Figure 2.20, notice that the two double leaves flank a triple-lobed leaf in the center.

The Root

The vast majority of baroque carvings have a beginning or "root" from which every leaf, scroll, and plane emanates. Figure 2.21a gives an example of the root. In Figure 2.21b notice that every line, leaf, and plane is traceable back to the root, in this case on the lower right.

Figure 2.21b. The root in context

Combinations

In Figure 2.22, notice the way in which two double-lobed leaves can be combined to create a scroll. Figure 2.23 is a similar example with the addition of lobes on the outside curve. It creates an entirely different effect.

The following are examples of similar leaf combinations with different treatments of the leaf ends. The effects realized are remarkably different. Figure 2.24a shows a series of double-lobes with a curled leaf tip while Figure 2.24b shows a similar leaf with a scroll at the end.

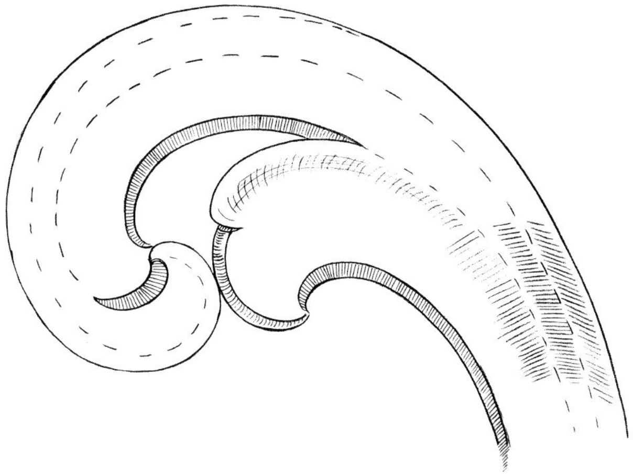

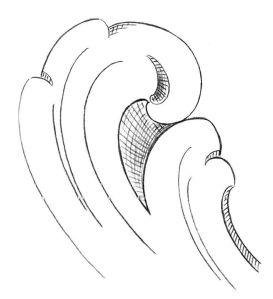

Figure 2.22. Combination of two double-lobed leaves

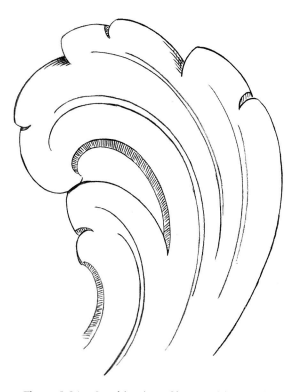

Figure 2.24a. Combination of leaves with curled leaf tip

Figure 2.23. Combination of three double-lobed leaves

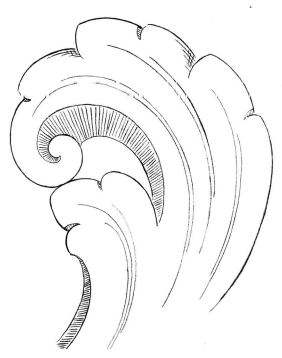

Figure 2.24b. Combination of leaves with a scroll leaf end

Folded Leaves

The folded leaf in Figure 2.25 has one double lobe folded lying on top of the rest of the leaf. Figure 2.26 is an example of the folded leaf combined with several other leaf types illustrating a very pretty detail on a scroll. Figure 2.27 shows a folded leaf abutting a curled leaf tip.

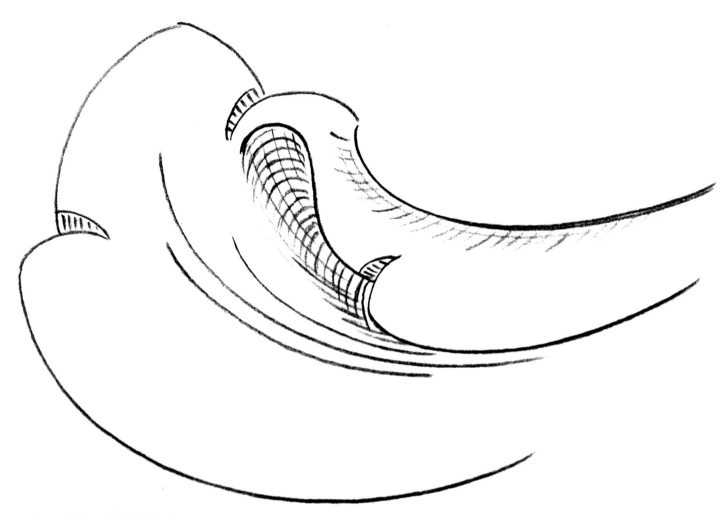

Figure 2.25. Folded leaf-basic

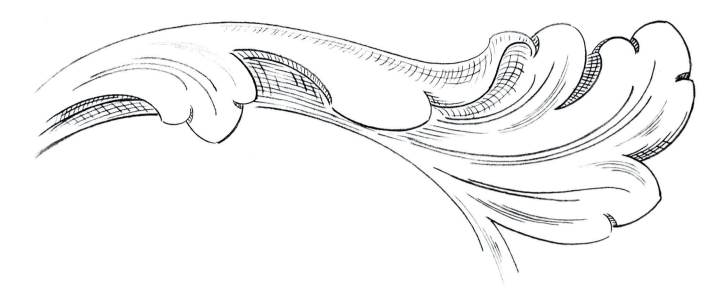

Figure 2.26. Folded leaf
in combination with
other leaves

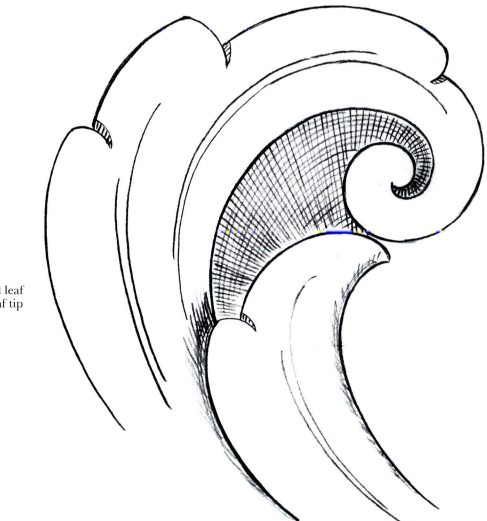

Figure 2.27. A folded leaf
abutting a scrolled leaf tip

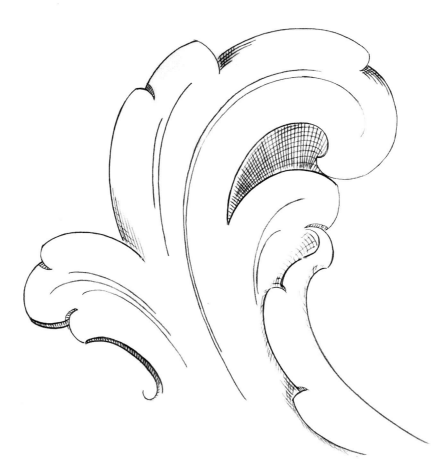

Figure 2.28. Folded leaf next to a curled leaf tip

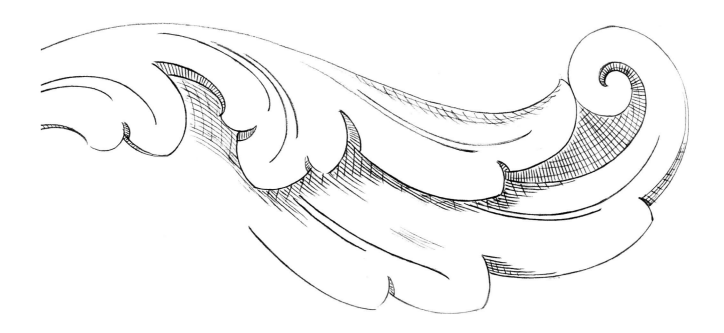

Figure 2.29. Combination of folds, scrolls and leaf types

Figure 2.28 demonstrates a folded leaf abutting a curled tip. The combination of a folded leaf and a scroll end with other leaves creates a very interesting and pleasing visual effect. (Figure 2.29)

Crossovers

If you were to take your thumb and cross it over your index finger, you would have resultant creases and a raised portion at the base of this crossover. The raised ridge is an accentuated, stylized crescent moon. In Figure 2.30 the smaller leaves have not yet crossed over the larger scroll but the ridge and crescent moon folds are apparent. In the example shown in Figure 2.31, the leaf tips may just be touching, but the telltale folds and crescent moons come into play. Figure 2.32 shows the leaf lying on top of the scroll creating a nice three-dimensional effect and lovely shadows. This is where different levels impart interest to the piece. The example shown in Figure 2.33 illustrates that the outside leaves start toward each other, which makes the triple leaf in the center fold back. The triple is hanging down in this case and vaguely resembles a flower. This detail adds much interest and can be seen on numerous pieces of furniture and in architecture. Figure 2.34 illustrates a stem crossover. Notice that crossovers will occur elsewhere in the carving with vastly differing results.

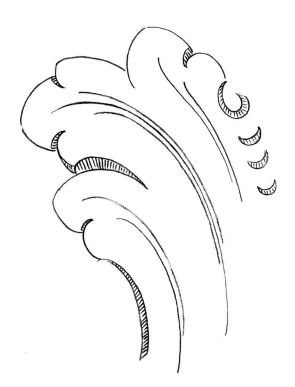

Figure 2.31. Leaves touching each other

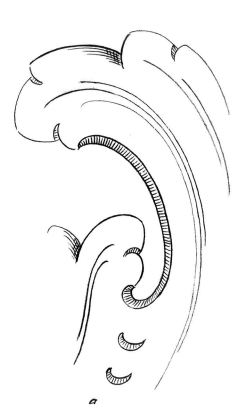

Figure 2.30. Leaves approaching crossing over

Figure 2.32. Cross over with different levels

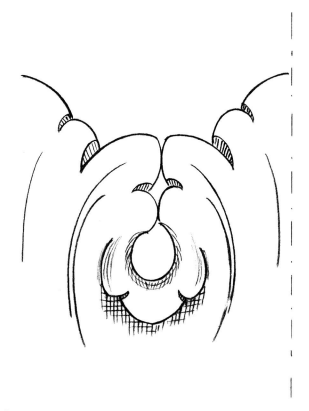

Figure 2.33. Cross over with center folded back

Figure 2.34. Stem crossing over

Flowers

Flowers have many forms in baroque and rococo carving styles. The following examples show how a minor change in the petal tips can have a major influence on the overall design. Figure 2.35 shows a flower with curled petal tips. Figure 2.36 illustrates a flower with stylized scroll petal ends.

With the basics firmly in hand, you can start drawing patterns and elements before proceeding to the actual carving.

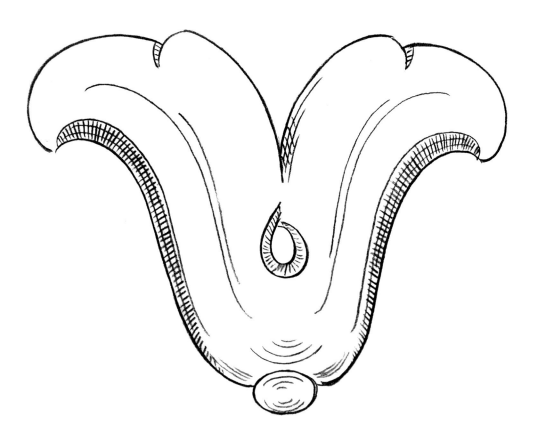

Figure 2.35. Flower design with plain tips

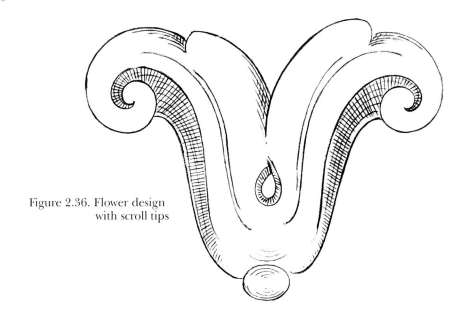

Figure 2.36. Flower design with scroll tips

Chapter 3
Preparation

Proper Preparation
Makes Carving Easier and Quicker

Good wood is the basis of good carvings. The acanthus style lends itself to basswood (linden wood or lyme), pine, oak, mahogany, walnut, and birch—basically any wood without pronounced grain. The grain on butternut and other woods, although easily carved, will distract from the flow of the curves.

3.1. Wood Preparation

Wood is best harvested in the winter when the sap is not flowing. If you are cutting your own trees, remove the bark immediately so that fungus does not start to grow in the wood. You can recognize wood that has not been harvested properly by blue streaks in the lumber (Figure 3.1a). Spalted wood is an advanced stage of fungus where the wood has turned blue and brown (Figure 3.1b). This is appropriate for woodturning, box making, and ornamental designs, but is generally unacceptable for carving because the coloring will be distracting and the wood is punky (too soft).

Figure 3.1b. Spalted wood

Figure 3.1a. Blue wood

Once the tree is felled, the wood is then rough sawn. The wood slabs are then stacked with "stickers" or pieces of wood between each board. This allows air to flow between each board so that the wood dries evenly. When stacking, be sure to allow for air between each piece from side to side. Make sure that the stickers are as small as possible and use more of them rather than less. A few large stickers might allow the wood to warp and the stickers themselves can leave marks or discoloration. Therefore, a small piece of the same species is preferable.

The wood should be allowed to dry for at least one year. Kiln dried wood is available and will give satisfactory results, but air-dried is superior in that it is less brittle. Note the shavings from a kiln dried piece (Figure 3.2a) verses an air-dried piece (Figure 3.2b).

The other way to cut a log is known as quarter-sawn. The reason for this name is that the log is quartered before it is sawn into flat planks. Figure 3.4 illustrates the way a quarter-sawn lumber is milled.

Figure 3.2a. Broken chips from kiln-dried wood

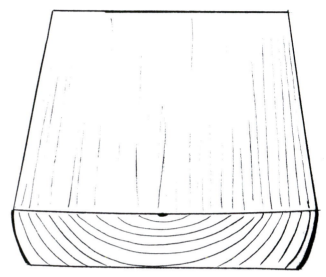

Figure 3.3. Flat sawn board

Figure 3.2b. Smooth shaving from air-dried wood

Notice that there are two different ways to saw logs. Flat sawn logs yield wood that generally has curved end grain, as shown in Figure 3.3. Flat sawn boards with the "C" type of end grain might yield a cupped board as it dries.

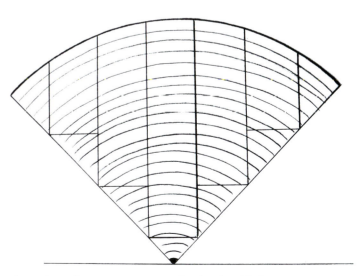

Figure 3.4. The way quarter sawn lumber is milled

The resultant planks have vertical end grain (Figure 3.5) and tend to be more stable. These boards will stay flat more readily. Regardless of how the wood is initially sawn, the heartwood will be removed (Figure 3.6). Boards that are glued-up without heartwood have more consistent color, reduced cracking and checking, and carve more consistently.

Now you have a pile of air-dried lumber. The first thing to do is to sight along the boards to check for bows, twists, hooks, and cupping (Figures 3.7a-c). If a board has a hook at one end, cut it off.

Figure 3.7a. Bowed board

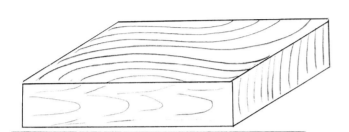

Figure 3.5. The resultant vertical end grain from quarter sawn lumber

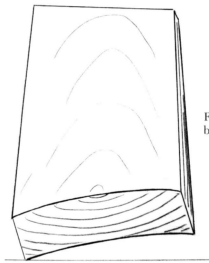

Figure 3.7b. Twisted board

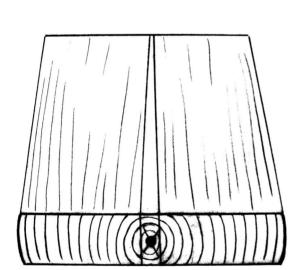

Figure 3.6. Remove the heartwood for best results

Figure 3.7c.
Cupped board

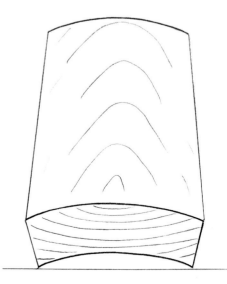

A board that is not flat can be planed as often as you like and it will not straighten. If any of the above defects are very pronounced, it will be advantageous to cut the board into shorter pieces. At this point you may want to cut out any knots, since they are tough on the planer, jointer, and saw blades.

The pieces may now be placed on a jointer to flatten or straighten one edge or surface. Once a reference edge or face is established, the opposite edges can be cut or planed and will remain parallel. You should end up with some very fine pieces of lumber with which to proceed.

3.2. Gluing Up

Many times patterns require pieces of wood that need to be glued for size or depth. If possible, boards should be glued with a good permanent wood glue. Epoxies are fine, but can chip the edge of a chisel. Dowels, biscuits, and other forms of reinforcement are generally unnecessary and are to be avoided so that you do not discover them when carving. If possible, stay away from metal fasteners. In many antiques, it has been found that metal rusts and destroys the wood immediately surrounding it.

There are some general rules when gluing. When gluing up flat panels, use vertical grain wood whenever possible (Figure 3.8a). Alternate the direction of the grain when gluing so that the panel remains relatively flat (Figure 3.8b). This prevents the panel from cupping or warping.

There are many patterns that require extra depth in spots. In those pieces, it is fine to glue an extra block to the wood (Figure 3.9a - c). If possible, stagger the joints. Figure 3.9a shows how two flat panels should be oriented when gluing up. To glue up a large block, notice the orientation of the grain (Figure 3.9b). This is less likely to split or change shape than a large piece of wood. Additionally, large pieces are often hollowed to lessen the likelihood of cracking or splitting. Staggering the joints when adding depth creates additional strength (Figure 3.9c).

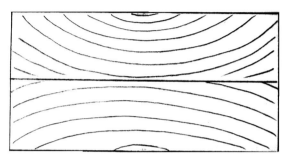

Figure 3.9a. Grain direction for gluing flat panels

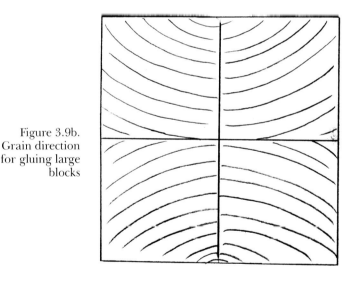

Figure 3.9b. Grain direction for gluing large blocks

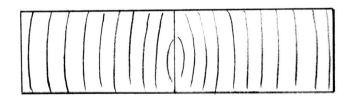

Figure 3.8a. Boards with vertical grain side by side

Figure 3.8b. Boards with alternating grain

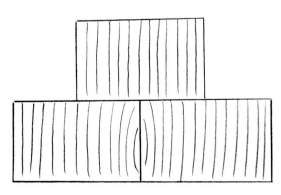

Figure 3.9c. Staggered joints

The wrong way to glue up is by crisscrossing the grain, as illustrated in Figure 3.10. Cracks will develop over time.

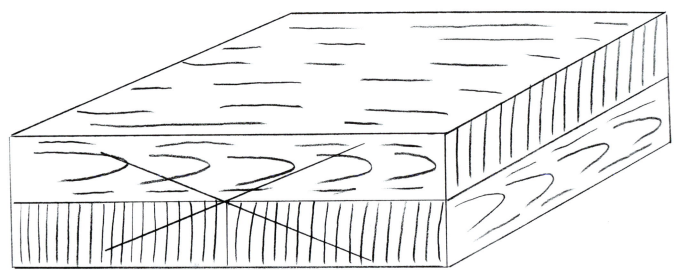

Figure 3.10. Wrong way to glue up

3.3. Cutting Out The Design

A timesaving device is to cut the profile of the pattern before gluing on the extra pieces (Figure 3.11a-c)

Figure 3.11a. Wood carving before addition.

Figure 3.11b. Pre-cut piece glued on.

Figure 3.11c.
Oblique view of
above.

Patterns can get quite confusing, especially when you carve off all of the lines establishing levels. It is therefore best to remove the areas that are not part of the finished carving first. Clearly mark them with and "X" before proceeding (Figure 3.12).

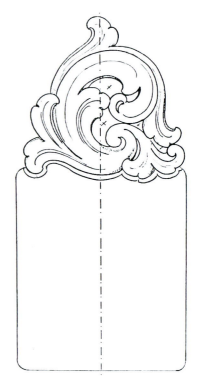

The places on the outside of the design can easily be removed with a scroll saw or a band saw. The interior sections must be carefully drilled and scroll-sawn or jig-sawn (Figures 3.13a - c). Be careful to stay away from the lines and leave some wood for clean-up while carving.

Figure 3.12. Pattern with X's clearly marked

Figure 3.13a. Scroll saw cutting the exterior of the pattern

Figure 3.13b. Band saw cutting the exterior of the pattern.

Figure 3.13c. Scroll saw cutting the interior of the pattern.

Cut out or "pierced" carvings may stand alone or can be glued to a substrate as seen on countless pieces of furniture, frames, and architectural elements.

An alternate approach is to have a bas-relief where the carving is above the board and the background is dropped down with a router. Unless you are doing production, this is done freehand by carefully following the pattern. This is dangerous in that routers tend to grab. Therefore, it is necessary to make small cuts by lowering the bit a little with each pass. Leave plenty of room around the carving (Figure 3.14a-c). This is only a timesaving device and may be skipped altogether. The carving would then be shaped entirely by hand. There should be no visible difference in the finished product either way.

Figures 3.14a-c.
Pattern being routed

3.4. Roughing Out

In many instances, the face of the carving will be domed or rounded (Figure 3.15a). In other instances, the board may have a routed or planed shape (Figure 3.15b), or even be a full round (Figure 3.15c).

Regardless of the design, it is always best to establish the overall shape of the carving before you begin any detailing. A flat carving is not nearly as interesting as a contoured piece. Once the overall shape is established, sketch the pattern onto the wood again and start carving.

Look around you; there are excellent examples of carved acanthus in art, architecture, and furniture. These sources of inspiration are everywhere. You might enjoy going on a treasure hunt to discover how many examples of acanthus carving you can find. Keep a photo journal of the different styles and elements of acanthus that exist. These photos might serve as study or reference guides in the future.

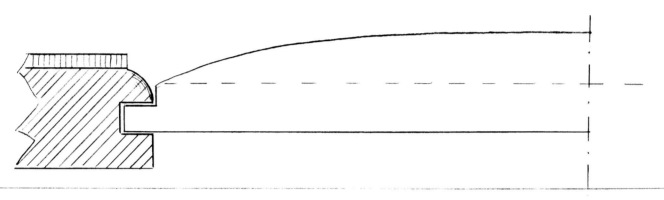

Fig. 3.15a. Domed panel

Fig. 3.15b. Shaped board for moldings, trim, and frames

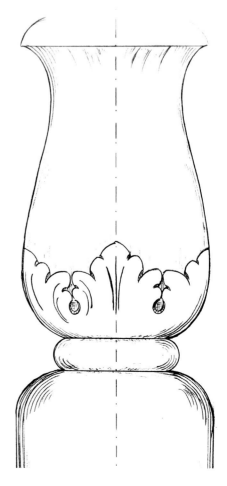

Fig. 3.15c. Turned full round piece for leg, candle holder or lamp

Chapter 4

Tool Care and Sharpening

The Key to Successful Carving is Sharp Tools

Ashley Isles, a carving tool manufacturer in Britain, once said, "You cannot learn how to carve, only how to sharpen." Although you can learn how to carve, his point is well taken; you cannot carve without a sharp tool. It is with this in mind that we lead off with the basics of sharpening before the carving techniques are revealed.

4.1. What is a Sharp Tool?

It is surprising to discover the number of carvers who have never experienced a truly sharp tool. Developing the ability to recognize a sharp tool is the right place to start.

A sharp tool will "sing" as it passes through the wood and not leave "comet trails." These trails look like faint lines created by barely perceptible nicks in the tools cutting edge. The lines follow the tool's path. With very sharp tools, you can get a mirror finish in the wood without lines or imperfections. Sandpaper would only destroy the quality of the finish. Sandpaper will remove the crisp lines, and the residual abrasive left in the wood will dull your tools quickly.

4.2. How to Spot and Test a Sharp Tool

Initially, if you sight along the sharp edge of your tool with a good light source above and your finger on the far side to reflect the light, the edge will appear as a single edge. There will be no breaks in the light or bright spots (Figure 4.1a). Any interference with a crisp edge indicates a spot that needs attention (Figure 4.1b). Remember, you can spot hone your tool. It is not necessary to regrind the entire tool every time; honing will suffice. Grinding will only shorten the tool length

quicker. There are times when you will need to regrind the entire tool. This may be due to a large knick or chip. Also, if honing rounds the bottom of your tool, regrinding will be necessary to establish a concave or flat bottom to the tool. Other than nicks and chips, there may be a portion of the tool that is dull throughout. To correct that area, sight along the edge and notice the portion of the edge that acts like a mirror and reflects the light to the eye (Figure 4.1c).

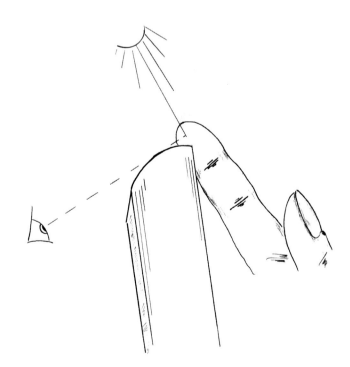

4.1a. A sharp tool with no breaks, glints or bright spots in the light on the edge.

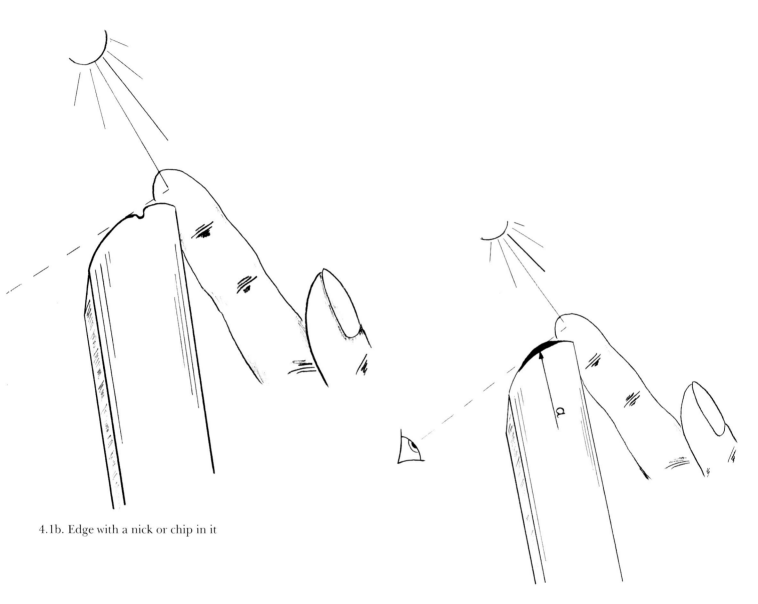

4.1b. Edge with a nick or chip in it

Fig. 4.1c. The flat portion of the edge reflects the light to reveal the area that needs to be ground.

Some people test a tool by scraping it along the back of a fingernail and others test by shaving with it. The problem with these methods is that they do not test the entire edge. Most importantly, the tool must be tested on a piece of scrap wood so that you can be certain that the entire edge leaves a clean cut. Cut across the grain and look for a mirror finish on the wood. That's what you are looking for. Now, how do you get it?

If you can shape wood, you can shape metal. Sharpening metal is like sculpting with a grinder. The result is a tool that you use to sculpt wood. Achieving a beautiful shape to the tool takes practice and is well worth the effort.

Tools were originally manufactured and supplied rough ground so that carvers could endow their tools with whatever bevel or profile they desired. Now tools are honed and ready to use. The advantage is that you can use them immediately. The disadvantage is that it prevents the carver from shaping and sharpening the tool, thereby claiming ownership of its edge. For example, you can use the correct bevel for the wood you will be carving. You can also change the shape of the tip to fit the need of the tool.

4.3. Rough Grinding and Shaping the Edge — Types of Bevels

The most critical component to rough grinding is that the tool remains cool and does not overheat. If the tool is overheated, it requires an enormous amount of work to correct it. With this in mind, I keep my fingers on the top of the tool near the edge. This way I can be certain that the tool's bevel is riding flat on the sharpening surface and that the tool remains cool.

If a tool does overheat, you will see a black spot along the edge (Figure 4.2). This is burnt metal with no carbon in it. Therefore, the edge has been depleted of its strength. The only way to correct this is to slowly grind away the burn marks, keeping the tool cool by frequently letting it cool in air or by dipping it into water. If sharpening many tools at once, an oil-based mister can be used; this sprays onto the grinding wheel, lubricating the wheel as it cools the tool.

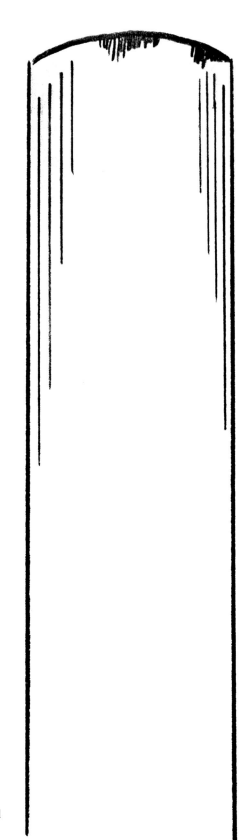

Fig. 4.2. Burnt spot on tool

When shaping a tool by grinding, try not to get overzealous by grinding off the corners (Figure 4.3) Use a light touch on the wheel. Let the wheel do the work and lift the corners as you pass the tool over the grinder. Remember, the corners have the least amount of steel to conduct the heat away. You need to grind a steeper bevel to cut through harder woods. This bevel is approximately 30° (Figure 4.4). For softer woods, a 25° bevel will suffice (Figure 4.5).

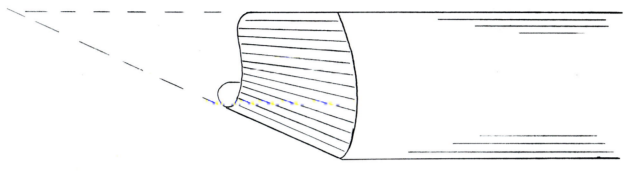

Fig. 4.3. Do not round the corners

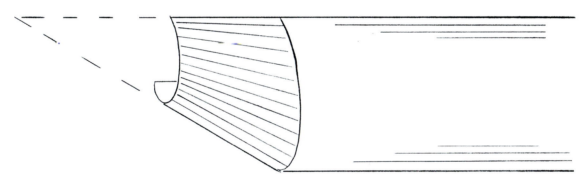

Fig. 4.4. Tool with a 30° bevel for harder woods

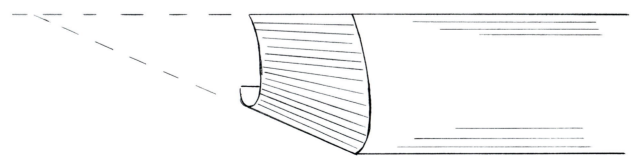

Fig. 4.5. Tool with a 25° bevel for softer woods

Some carvers prefer to include a shorter bevel on the outside of the tool at the tip, strengthening the tip and reducing chatter. This bevel is optional but very effective (Figure 4.6). You will also notice in the same illustration a "micro-bevel" on the inside of the tool. This allows you to turn the tool upside down without digging in.

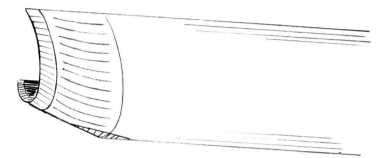

Fig. 4.6. Tool with short bevel outside & micro-bevel inside

Another detail when shaping a tool by grinding is to remove its heel (Figures 4.7a & b). This reduces drag when carving and allows access to tight spots. Although removing the heel is also optional, it will serve you well in acanthus and ornamental carving.

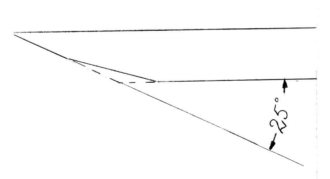

Fig. 4.7a. Tool for softer woods with heel removed

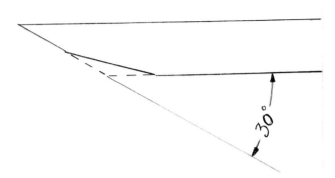

Fig. 4.7b. Tool for harder woods with heel removed

Once again, the tool would have a micro-bevel on top (Figure 4.8). Without the micro-bevel, the tool would tend to dig in when turned upside down (Figure 4.9a). With a micro-bevel, the tool will cut nicely (Figure 4.9b). It is especially useful to be able to reverse tools that have a curved cutting edge (Sheffield numbers 3 – 11). See the Sheffield Chart (page 125). Flipping the tool over allows you to shape convex and concave surfaces with the same tool.

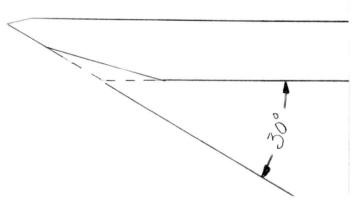

Figure 4.8. Tool with heel removed and micro-bevel on top.

Figure 4.9a. The tool without a micro-bevel on top will dig in when flipped over.

Figure 4.9b. A micro-bevel allows the tool to be used up or down.

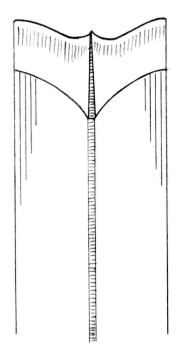

Figure 4.10b. Both sides are sharpened and there is a projection at the bottom.

Grinding V-tools (parting tools) sometimes stymies carvers. By breaking the V-tool into its components, you can very easily approach it successfully. View the V-tool as two adjacent flat chisels connected by a tiny curved chisel. Grind each flat side first, keeping the edge perpendicular to the wheel. The bottom of the V will look one of three ways (Figures 4.10a – c). If both sides meet perfectly, move directly to honing. If one wing is tilting forward or back, you did not have the edge perpendicular to the wheel. As in Figure 4.10b, if there is a projection at the bottom, you must gently roll the bottom of the tool on the grinder until the projection disappears. If, on the other hand, you are missing the bottom of the V, then, very carefully, grind back each side until it meets the existing portion of the V at the bottom (Figure 4.10c). At this point you can hone and produce a very clean cut.

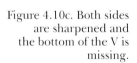

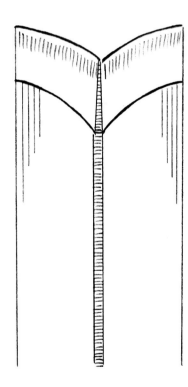

Figure 4.10c. Both sides are sharpened and the bottom of the V is missing.

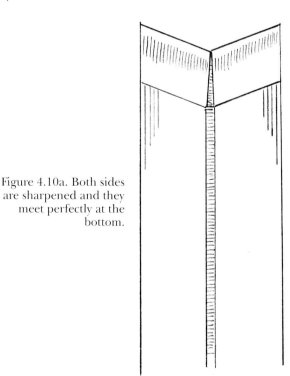

Figure 4.10a. Both sides are sharpened and they meet perfectly at the bottom.

Lastly, there are three ways to contour a V-tool. The most popular is to have each wing perpendicular to the top edge of the tool (Figure 4.11a). You may also cut back the bottom of the V, mimicking two adjacent skew chisels (Figure 4.11b). This tool will cut through the wood beautifully, but you must be cognizant of the pointy wing tips at all times. They can dig into a protruding feature very readily. The last way to profile a V-tool is to have the bottom of the V extend beyond the rest of the tool (Figure 4.11c). This tool will be used very rarely in that it will tend to dig in. It is only useful in detailing and getting into places that other tools can not reach.

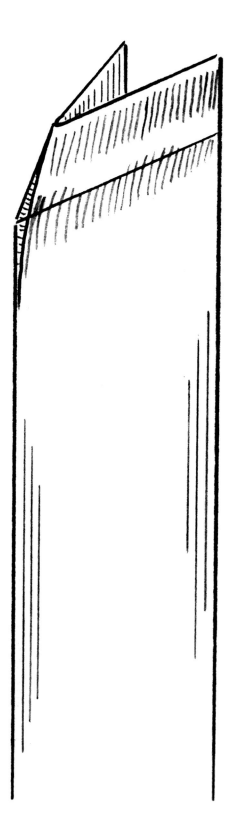

Figure 4.11a. Tool with a perpendicular end.

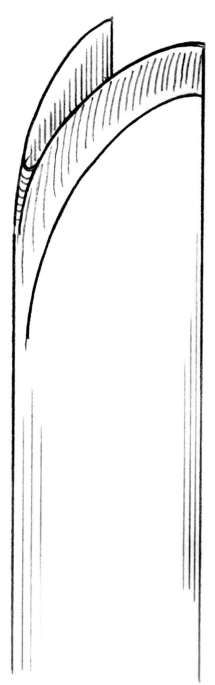

Figure 4.11b. Tool with the bottom of the V-cut back.

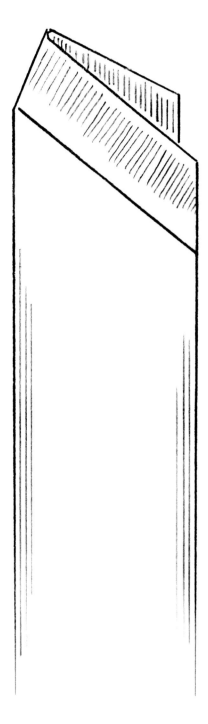

Figure 4.11c. Tool with the bottom of the V as the leading edge.

4.4. Honing

Once the tool has the profile and the desired angles, it needs to be honed to a finished edge. Again, when the tool has a proper edge, it will travel across the grain without leaving tear-out or "comet" trails. Test the sharpness on a piece of scrap wood before committing it to finishing a carving.

Many people use different compounds and methods for honing. Leather straps on a hard surface or rubber honing sticks all work well. You can use aluminum oxide powder, paste or wax sticks with embedded compound. All are effective. The only critical component is that you have your honing items close at hand and do it often while carving. You will not have to grind as often, only when a nick or inability to cut occurs. Honing is a continuous process during carving.

Some carvers use a wheel to hone the edge. Leather wheels, paper wheels, wood wheels, and hard felt wheels all work well (Figure 4.12).

Notice that soft wheels (e.g. cotton buffing wheels) will give you a honed sharp edge, but the tool pushes into the wheel. The resultant shape is a curved bottom tool with a sharp edge (Figure 4.13).

You will be wondering why a sharp tool will not cut at all. As you round the bottom of the tool, the tool becomes sharp with a very blunt angle. A tool like this would be like trying to cut wood with a cold-chisel for steel. At best, if the tool does cut with a rounded bottom, you will not be able to have it track well. The resultant carving will have wavy lines instead of smooth, flowing surfaces. As such, you will need to regrind the tool and pay attention to the method used to hone. In so doing, you will want to retain a flat or slightly concave bottom to the tool.

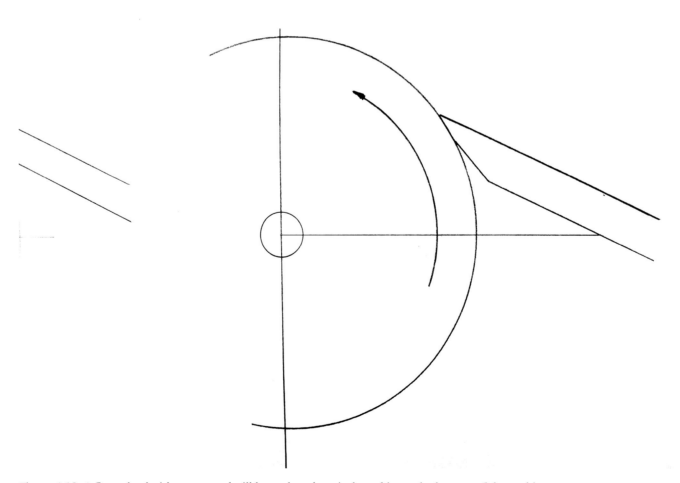

Figure 4.12. A firm wheel with compound will hone the edge nicely and leave the bottom of the tool intact.

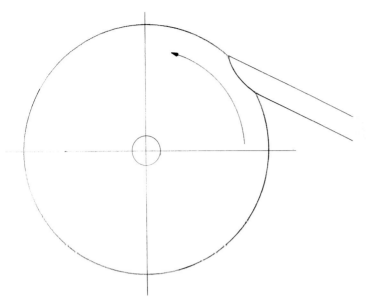

Figure 4.13. Notice that a soft buffing wheel will hone the edge, but create a rounded bottom tool that is impossible to use.

4.5. Care of Tools

As the old saying goes, an ounce of prevention is worth a pound of cure. By keeping a light film of oil or wax on the surface, the tools will not rust. There are many synthetic products that are available as well. Although there are all kinds of claims from manufacturers, any protective coating is fine. The only product to avoid is one with silicone in it. Transferring the silicone from the tool to the carving will virtually guarantee difficulty with any type of finish that you apply.

Should you find rust on the tool, careful polishing typically removes rust. Ink erasers work well. Some chemical rust removers work well, too. The only important thing to remember is that you must be diligent in removing all of the rust. Any remaining rust tends to attract water (hydrophilic), which promotes more rust. A clean surface is one where moisture will roll off or wipe off easily. Pits in the metal are a great place for water to lodge, so be thorough in cleaning the tool's surface.

4.6. Handles

If a handle becomes cracked or the tool comes without a handle, it is always nice to be familiar with how to replace them. If you make them from scratch, use different types of wood so that you can differentiate your tools quickly as you are carving.

All handles require a ferrule so that the handle will not crack as force is applied to the tool. A ferrule is a tube that is placed around the neck of the handle. When sliding a ferrule onto the outside of the handle, you can punch a dimple in it to securely hold it on.

To shape the handle, you can put it on the lathe or shape flat surfaces with a sander. The advantage to flat surfaces on the handle is that the tool will not roll off the bench.

When drilling the handle to accept the tool, stand the handle vertically in a drill press or secure it in a vice to use a hand drill. Most carving tools have tapered tangs that fit into the handle. Note that the tang and base of the tool are not hardened. This is so that they will not crack under pressure. The hole should be tapered and slightly undersized to grip the tool securely. To taper the hole, drill as series of holes, each one deeper and smaller. If the drill is not perfectly in alignment with the handle, the tool will mount crooked. This tool will be difficult to carve with and it will very likely break at the base of the tool. So, be certain to drill carefully for a satisfactory result. Place a hardwood block on the end of the tool and gently tap it into the handle. When fitting larger handles to larger tools, many of the old-time carvers put a leather washer between the base of the tool and the handle. This absorbs some of the impact when pounding on the handle and potentially adds to the life of the handle and the tool.

4.7. Transporting Tools Safely

There are toolboxes, tool rolls, tubes, corks, and any number of ways to transport tools safely. Be certain to protect the edges from touching any other metal since they are hardened and brittle, so any encounter will surely result in a nick or chip. Remember, it takes seconds to hone an edge of a tool, but much longer to reshape or grind it before honing.

Test your leather or corks before using them to protect your tools. Certain leathers are tanned in such a way as to be corrosive to tools. When using old wine corks to protect tool steel, the chances are good that it may corrode the steel as well. Heavy weight canvas tool rolls are effective and rugged. Whatever your method of protecting the tools, once again, be diligent about preventive maintenance.

4.8. Conclusion

There is no single correct way to shape, sharpen, hone or store tools. Everyone has different ideas. As long as your system works for you, makes carving easier and a joy to accomplish, you are ahead of the game. Of course, the quicker methods of sharpening and honing are preferred, as they leave more time for carving.

Chapter 5
Getting Started

It Is Easier Than You Think

After the pattern is transferred onto the wood and the lines are cleaned up, the first step is to outline the piece with a chisel.

While reading this chapter, you may want to refer to the chisel shapes, which are described on the Sheffield Chart (page 125).

5.1. Outlining and Stop Cuts

An easy way to start is by outlining the piece with vertical stop cuts by cutting straight down along the pencil lines. This vertical cut serves to prevent pieces of wood from chipping out as you clean up the areas around the pattern. They literally "stop" the cut from going too far. Be sure not to undercut any of the parts of the carving at this point. By not undercutting any areas, you can adjust the heights of different areas without changing the shape or size of any of the elements.

There are a number of ways to outline. One way is to push straight down with a chisel that approximates the curve that you would like to replicate. Of course, you may want to use a mallet, but be certain not to go too deep. Another way to outline the curves is to hold the chisel upright and tilt it back on one corner. You can now slice through the wood as if you are water skiing or snow skiing. By turning the handle above, you can steer and tighten or relax the radius of the curve (Figure 5.1). Notice that the chisel is tilted back. The heel of the cutting edge is dug in and the leading edge is out of the wood. The shape of the curve for the stop-cut is controlled by steering from up above.

Figure 5.1. Vertical chisel being pushed through the pattern.

There is always the trusty V-tool (parting tool), which you may use to outline. A veiner (the shape of a letter U or #11 tool) is also useful for wasting away wood from outside of the pattern.

Once the pattern is outlined, the remaining wood must be brought down to the level of the background. A skew chisel (#2) or slightly curved chisel (#3 or #4) will work fine for this. A spoon bent tool allows you to get into spaces between raised elements (Figure 5.2).

Be certain to leave a thin layer of wood throughout the background to clean up at the very end. This will remove any stray marks that might have occurred.

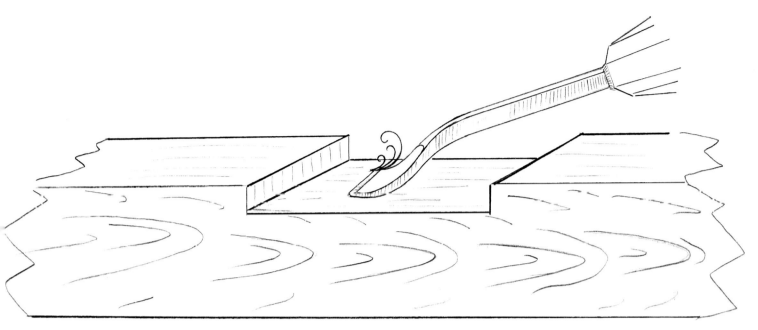

Figure 5.2. Leveling the background with a spoon bent chisel

5.2. Grain Direction

When carving acanthus leaves and scrolls, you will be crossing different directions of grain many times. You must always be cognizant of the grain and work with it and not fight it. This is where extremely sharp tools are a must. By ignoring the grain, the wood will win and happily chip out. If you work with the wood, it will reward you with beautiful scrolls featuring a mirror finish. Remember, "sand" is a four-letter word. Sanding will only obliterate detail. The surface will never be as smooth, shiny, and crisp as the appearance of a chiseled result.

When carving the outside of a spiral or circle, the grain will behave differently every 90°. The insides of the curves and outside curves also behave differently (Figure 5.3). This is known as the "donut rule." Always carve with the grain: as you carve the inside or outside of a circle, you will have to change the direction of the tool four times.

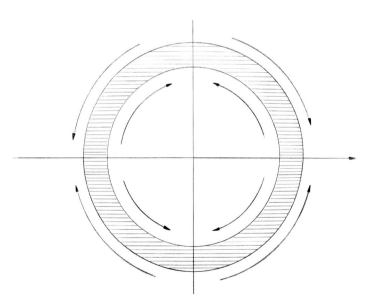

Figure 5.3. The "donut rule"

The rule of thumb is to treat the wood as if you are petting a dog or cat. If you pet in the direction of the fur, the animal will be happy. But ruffle the fur and watch out. By the same token, if you carve along the grain and not against it you will never go wrong (Figure 5.4a). Be certain to have stop-cuts pre-established so that you do not remove a chip from the entire face. There are times when using a V-tool or a veiner (#11, U-shape) that one side of the cut is with the grain and the opposite side is cutting against the grain (Figures 5.4b & c). In this case, carve in one direction and then reverse the direction of the cut and lean the tool toward the wall that needs to be cleaned up. Both sides of the cut will appear clean and smooth.

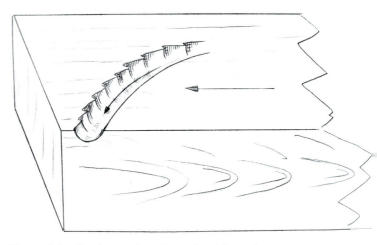

Figure 5.4c. Carving against the grain with a veiner

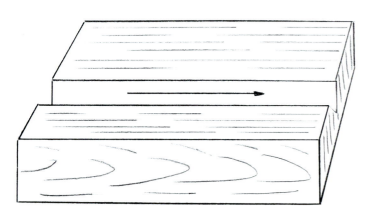

Figure 5.4a. Carving with the grain.

Figure 5.4b. Carving against the grain with a V-tool

Always be careful along the outer edges that you do not chip off details. By paying special attention to the grain, the chances are minimized.

Scrolls often loop above and below each other. When establishing different levels, always carve downhill toward a valley (Figure 5.5). This is as if you are snow skiing. If you carve uphill, the chances that you lift off a section of the carving increase dramatically.

Figure 5.5. Side-view carving with chisels working downhill towards a valley.

Avoid removing areas that might be needed later. In other words take down each area in stages. As you adjust the heights of one area, you may need to adjust the height of an adjacent area to create proper flow.

5.3. Establishing Levels & Planes

It is important to establish different levels, planes, and the overall shape before you start detailing any leaves or scrolls. The temptation is enormous to see how a certain portion will look. It is a shame to have perfect leaves and discover later on that they have to be removed to fit into the overall scheme of the carving. Rough carve the entire piece to establish levels before any finished carving is done.

The best way to establish planes on the outside of the scroll is to start at the bud (leaf tip) and work back toward the root. Notice that there are always three planes in view on the outside of the scroll. When a leaf from the inside of the scroll is added, a plane is dropped out of sight from the outside of the scroll. The appearance is that the plane rolled out of sight toward the back of the carving. This creates an illusion of flow from the back of the carving which does not actually exist (Figure 5.5a).

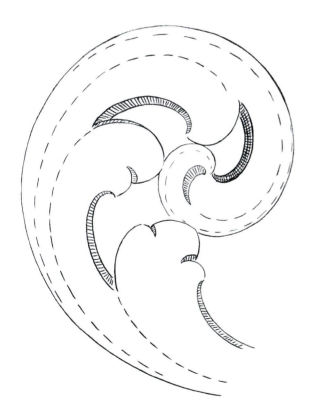

Figure 5.5a.

5.4. Creating Motion & Flow

Once the overall heights are determined, it is necessary to define and refine the motion or flow of the piece. Typically, in acanthus carving, the design starts from the root and emanates from there. See Figures 2.21a & b in Chapter 2 (page 18).

Any element of the carving can be traced directly back to the root. Flowing out from the root should be a smooth continuous journey. You can imagine yourself sailing along on a roller coaster or entering a highway on a ramp. Either way the curves are smooth, gentle, and continuous. There are no sharp corners or jerky twists and turns, no sudden drops; only smooth gradual transitions.

If you look at historic carvings, the flow is often similar to flowing hair, fur or feathers. Everything blends effortlessly without sharp bends. The motion of the material is smooth and soothing to the eye.

5.5. Types of Cuts & Tool Control

In order to get smooth, flowing, continuous curves, it may be necessary to think of your carving tools in a very different light. For example, you might find yourself using a flat chisel to make some very fancy curves. Alternatively, you may find yourself carving with your tools standing straight up or even upside down. All of these techniques will be described below.

In order to rough out shapes, levels, and planes, and create flow, it is often easiest to use a flat or nearly flat tool (#2 skew or #3). The flat tool is generally a skew chisel because it makes a slicing motion as it moves along the surface of the wood (Figure 5.6).

Figure 5.6. Establishing planes on scrolls with a flat chisel (#1) or a skew (#2)

If you define rough shapes with a number three gouge, you will find it useful, in spots, to turn the tool over to define some soft outer surfaces of the scrolls (Figure 5.7).

Figure 5.7. Tool upside down producing curved surfaces.

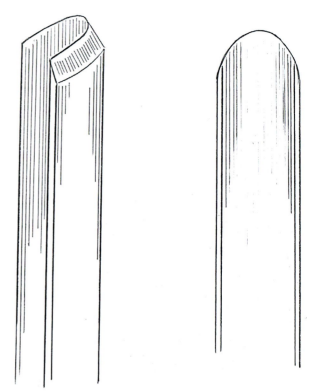

Figure 5.9. Tool with a negative rake on the end

For creating crescent moon shapes where stems or leaves fold over each other (Figure 5.8), it is often helpful to have a negative rake on the end of the tool (Figure 5.9).

To make "eyes," where the leaves look as though they are unfolding (Figure 5.10a-b), some carvers prefer a slightly rounded profile to the end of the tool. This is so the tool may change directions more readily when it is being held upright (Figure 5.11).

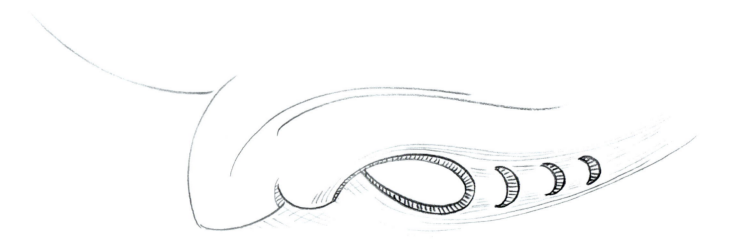

Figure 5.8. "Crescent moons" representing creases in the fold

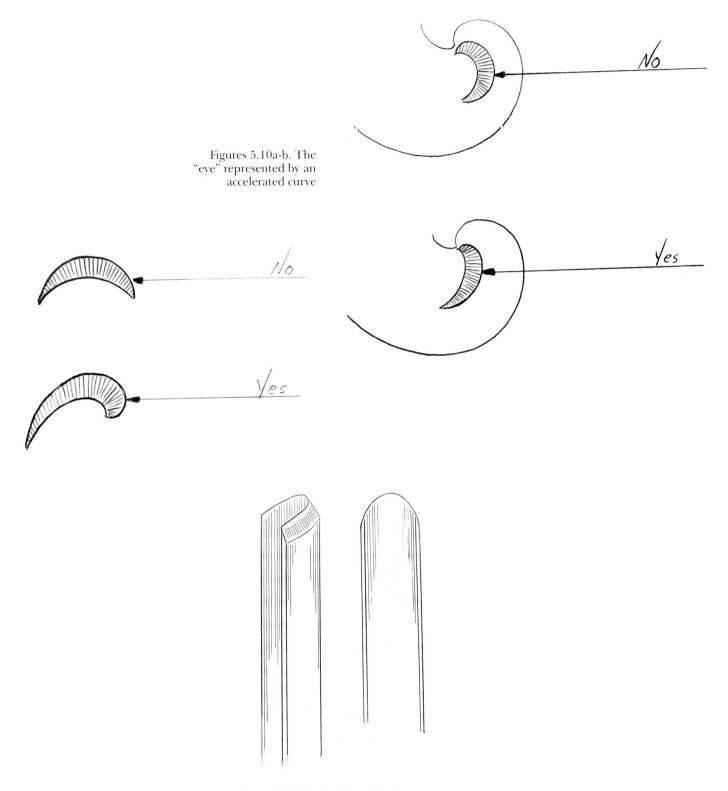

Figures 5.10a-b. The "eye" represented by an accelerated curve

Figure 5.11. Tool with a slightly rounded end

5.6. Creating Shadow

Once the carving is completed to your satisfaction, it is time for the final steps, which include undercutting to add shadow. You must be certain that you are happy with the levels, planes, and flow before adding shadow. This process starts with undercutting certain areas of the carving. As such, you will no longer be able to go back and change the levels without losing leaf tips or other details. When you undercut, the idea is to fool the eye into seeing light, feathery edges without affecting the integrity of the carving (Figure 5.12). From the front, the leaf appears to have a delicate edge. From the side, it can be seen that the leaf edge is pronounced, but there is plenty of material beneath it. The additional mass supporting the leaf makes it less likely to crack off. The edge implies a delicate, thin leaf without it actually being so. In Figure 5.13, you can see how a slight undercut as part of the last steps adds shadow so that the elements appear to float above the background.

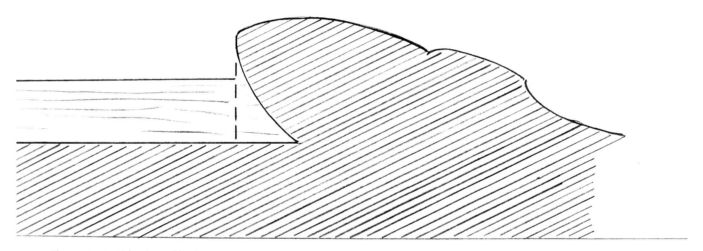

Figure 5.12. Side view of leaf tip

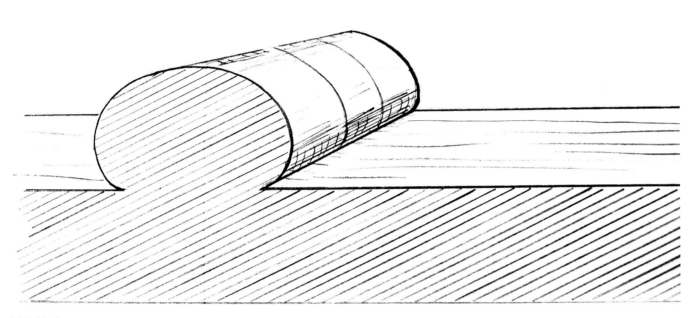

Figure 5.13. Undercut stem

This is a form of "*trompe-l'œil*" or "fool the eye." It is noted in painting with forced perspective, but applies equally well to carving. Leaves and scrolls appear to roll out from the back of the carving and some leaves look as if they are floating. In fact everything is well grounded and, often, the back of the scrolls are only implied and never really exist.

5.7. Back Carving

The best way to bring life to a pierced carving is to carve away the back. A pierced carving has the areas between the leaves and the scrolls cut away. The time to back carve is after the carving is finished, before adding the leaf veins. Note the difference between the before and after back carving (Figures 5.14a & b). Before back carving, the panel appears thick. After back carving, the scrolls appear thin and light. The shadows created by removing the back give the scrolls an airy effect.

When carving the back, it is best to draw the pattern on the reverse side, connecting the carved parts before beginning. Also pencil from the front the thicknesses of the scrolls and leaves, which will be approximately 1/4" - 3/8" depending upon the size and thickness of the carving. The material to be removed may be approached from the face or the back of the carving.

Carving from the back is not only to add light and shadow, but it is also possible to clean up the flow of the scrolls. When viewed from the front, regardless of the angle of the view, the eye sees scrolls effortlessly flowing in and out of sight. At no point should a dead end or rough curve be encountered. See Steps 29 - 32 in Chapter 7 (pages 76 and 77), on carving the breadboard.

Figure 5.14a.
Piece before back
carving

Figure 5.14b. Piece
after back carving

Chapter 6
Detailing the Carving

How Carvings Spring to Life

6.1. Veining

Adding the veins, stripes, accent lines, or "*geiss fuss*" (goat's foot) lines brings a great deal of finesse to the final result. These lines accentuate the curves and planes, and further imply parts of the scroll that do not exist. For example these lines might be emanating from the back of the carving where there is no scroll (Figure 6.1). These lines also follow the course of the planes established.

Figure 6.1.

Notice that the line weight varies along the leaf. It is thinnest at the base of the stem and gets fatter as it approaches the leaf tip. Generally, you start cutting at the leaf tip and lighten the touch as you approach the base of the leaf. With more than one lobe, the lines approach each other but never touch near the base of the stem. If they meet, the resultant line at the base would be thick and jumbled. Also note that the lines end at different points; they never line up in a row. The combination of lines fading out creates an illusion of a heavy weight line (combination of lines) getting lighter and lighter as it approaches the base of the stem. It eventually fades out before merging with another scroll.

6.2. Development of the Design Elements

Leaf Types

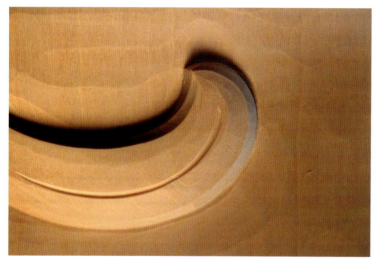

Figure 6.2. Single lobed leaf

Notice that the edges of the leaf have a bevel defining a thin edge.

Figure 6.3. Double lobed leaf

Here a concave plane runs along the inside edge. It does not end abruptly, but continues off the end of the leaf.

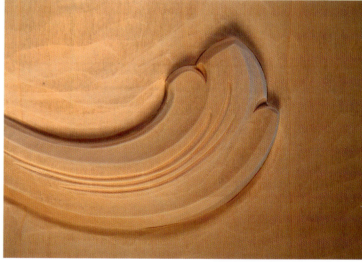

Figure 6.4. Triple lobed leaf

The smaller lobe trails behind the larger. The semi-circular nicks defining the outer and inner leaves end pointing back toward the veins and, ultimately, the root. Nothing points into outer space; rather it follows the planes and curves faithfully.

6.3. Stalks That Crossover

Typically, when two leaves or stems cross each other, the area puckers up, defining a raised ridge.

This ridge follows the curves and planes and fades
out as it approaches the root (Figure 6.5).

Figure 6.5. Crossover

To further accentuate the folding effect, little crescent moons are added. They are created with a #11 tool and follow the ridge exactly. In many historic carvings the crescent moon becomes a decorative element and trails off for quite some time. Each "moon" must get progressively smaller as you approach the root (Figure 6.6).

Figure 6.7. Leaf with fold on inside curve

Figure 6.6. Crossover with crescent moons

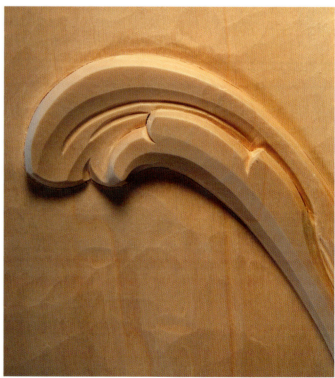

Figure 6.8. Leaf with fold on inside curve (different style)

6.4. Leaves That Roll Over

In the following examples you will notice that the leaves are folded over on the inside curve. The folds create nice shadows and enhance the dimensionality (Figures 6.7 - 6.9).

Figure 6.9. Leaf with fold on inside curve (2 lobes)

The leaves on the outside of a curve look as though they flop over from their own weight (Figure 6.10). The outside curve leaf may transition from fully open to folded over (Figure 6.11). Some outside curve leaves have a flip at the end of the leaf tip, creating a nice motion. The appearance is similar to that of a ski jump (Figure 6.12).

Figure 6.10. Fold on the outside of a curve

Figure 6.11. Fully open transitioning to fold

Figure 6.12. Ski jump leaf tip

Some leaves fold over completely upon themselves (Figure 6.13). This adds a delightful touch to an otherwise flat leaf. A few elements like this added to the overall carving perk up the piece enormously.

Figure 6.13. Leaf folding over itself

6.5. Decorative Elements

By careful examination of examples around you, you can spot unusual elements added to the design that create some unique effects. Examples include animals (dogs, lions, squirrels, snakes...) and people. Often you will find cherubs intertwined with the leaves. Sometimes mythical creatures appear, including dragons, gryphons, trolls, and others. Often flowers are incorporated. The acanthus plant itself has flowers, but most of the carved ones have been highly stylized. See the examples that follow (Figures 6.14 - 6.18):

Figure 6.14. Dragon

Figure 6.15. Flower
(rose)

Figure 6.16. Stylized
flower

Figure 6.17. Snake

Figure 6.18. Cherub

It is the details that bring any carving to life. The piece itself can take shape quickly, yet it is the final steps and clean up that take time. The reward of seeing a carving jump off the background is immense. Take your time to add shadows, undercuts, clean lines, veins, and the like.

A truly fine carving will only look richer with a finish applied. Sloppy work will show up more with a finish. So, take your time and enjoy the process.

The illustrations are very clear in this book. You might want to start by practicing drawing leaf shapes to set them in your mind before you start carving.

Chapter 7
Projects

Bread Board and Pierced Panel

7.1. Preparation

Before you begin, there are a number of pointers that are useful in carving acanthus scrolls and all ornamental carvings. This style of carving is generally performed while standing up. This allows you to swing around through the curves and establish nice continuous lines. This is much more difficult while seated. When standing, the bench should be about two inches below your elbow while your arm is bent. Preferably, there is room around the bench, so that you can view the piece from many angles. As you move around the piece, you will see areas that need to be refined, that you cannot see from other angles. This is both because of the difference in the light and shadows and that the piece will look different from different perspectives. As such, you will notice curves, scrolls, and leaves that need further attention, which would otherwise look fine from straight on.

Another important feature is lighting. Fluorescent lighting is general and soft. You will not be able to achieve the shadows that you need to properly complete the carving. A good approach is to have a swing arm lamp mounted to the bench. This will cast deep shadows and it can be moved around to change the shadows. As the shadows move, you will immediately notice areas that need to be cleaned up.

Some carvers use a lamp on each side of the bench. Any method you use to hold down the carving should allow you to easily change the position of the carving so that you can work on it from different sides and angles. There are quite a variety of hold-downs. All of them are fine providing that they do not leave marks on the piece. The one handed clamps with rubber pads work well. If the clamp would disturb delicate carvings, you can leave a tab on the carving to clamp to. This tab will be removed last after all of the delicate detailing is complete. When back carving, you can use the non-skid foam pads often seen in woodworking supply houses or the pads for dishes in the houseware section of most stores. The carving must be flipped over many times, thus it may be easier to work on a foam surface without using clamps. As you flip the carving back and forth regularly, you will spot areas that need to be reshaped or thinned that you cannot see from the top of the carving alone.

The above pointers will serve you well in completing the practice pieces that follow. If you choose to start by practicing each of the leaf types, this approach will guarantee superior results.

7.2. Bread Board

In the following photographs, you will be able to follow in detail the steps required to create a beautiful acanthus carving.

Steps

2. Scroll or band saw the outside of the pattern. Drill, then scroll saw or jig saw the interior. Be certain to leave a little wood beyond the pattern lines for clean up.

1. Transfer the pattern to the wood. Clean up and darken the pattern so that it is clear. Add an "X" to each part to be removed.

3. Use a V-tool to visually separate the carving from the board.

4. Continue to outline with the V-tool.

5. Reverse the tool. Be mindful of the grain. Remember the "donut rule."

6. Put the stop cuts in first to avoid tear out.

7. Approach the stop cut with your tool (#9 or #11).

8. Continue outlining with vertical stop cuts. Be certain not to undercut. Undercutting will change the shape of the carving as you carve down. Undercutting might also promote lifting the element out altogether.

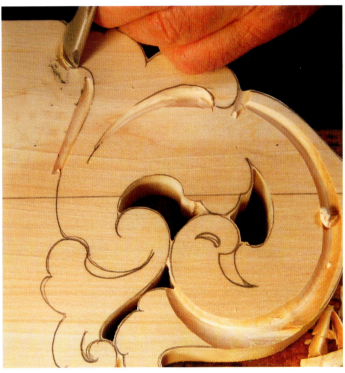

9. This cut defines half of the V bottom that follows the contour of the leaf.

10. Completing the cut: By approaching the cut from the opposite angle, the finished V is produced.

11. The tool "skis" through the wood with the heel dug in and the leading edge slightly above the wood. As such, the curve can be relaxed or tightened as the tool proceeds.

12. The tool defines the other side of the cut using the same technique.

13. The cut is set in with a stop cut.

14. The cut is completed, creating a V at the end of the leaf tip. Remember: do not undercut the leaf.

15. The root is defined with a stop cut that rolls around, following the curve.

16. The cut is then completed from the opposite angle.

17. The end of the inside leaf is set in with a sliding, vertical stop cut.

18. The cut is completed using the same motion from the opposite side.

19. More cuts to establish the outline of the carving. The first cuts create an edge that leans away from the carving and follows the shape of the leaf perimeter.

20. The clean up cuts meet at the bottom of the V-cut from the opposite side.

21. The planes are being established.

22. Continue establishing the planes, minding the grain (donut rule).

23. Define the outline of the main scroll by sliding the tool along the scroll's outer edge.

24. The skiing motion can tighten the curve as it progresses. This defines an accelerated curve.

25. The finished scroll outline.

26. The carving is cleaned up and ready for back carving.
Notice that if there is a sharp V-cut between the scroll and the adjacent leaves, they appear to emanate from the underside of the scroll. You can see this in the right side of the photo in Step 26. Whereas, if there is a soft curve (#9 or #11) between the leaves and the scroll, the leaves appear to roll off the scroll itself. You can see this on the left side of the photo in Step 26.

27. Before back carving, establish the thickness of the scroll from the front with a pencil. This should be approximately ¼"-3/8" depending on the size of the carving.

28. You can cut below this line from the top of the carving or carve to this line from the back.

29. Before proceeding, draw the overall shape of the scroll from the back so that you do not remove any needed elements as you back carve.

30. Start to thin out the leaves and scrolls.

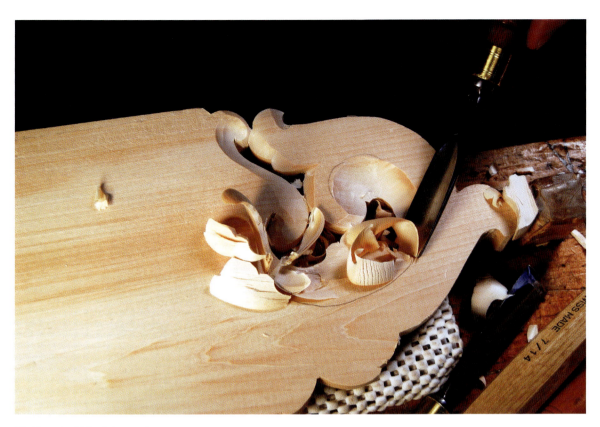

31. Be mindful of the grain.

32. Once the back carving is complete, the piece will appear light and airy from the front. The deep shadows resulting from back carving will give the leaves life, as they appear to float in space.

33. The carving can now be detailed by adding veins as described in the previous chapter.

34. The finished breadboard: Do not sand; it will only obliterate the detail. A coat of oil, wax or polyurethane will bring out the detail. It can also be sealed and painted (Chapter 8).

7.3. Pierced Panel

This type of panel would be appropriate for a cabinet door, box top or ornamental piece.

The steps are similar to the previous project so the annotations will be kept to a minimum. Study the photographs carefully so that you may get a sense of the flow and the order in which the carving evolves. For demonstration purposes, you can see unfinished areas next to finished areas. Typically, you would progress by roughing out the entire carving, establishing the appropriate levels and relationships. Then a process of refinement would occur. When satisfied with the results from the front, the carving is flipped over for back carving. If there are numerous levels, the back carving might be more time consuming than the front. After everything is cleaned up, the final detailing and veining is added.

Steps

1. In that this is a panel and not a completely cut out object, the center areas are removed with a scroll saw, and the outside is routed down to the background. Leave about 1/8˝ on the background to clean up after the rest of the carving is complete. Of course, the outside of the carving can be removed by hand instead of using a router; it just takes a little longer.

2. Clean up the perimeter of
the carving with vertical cuts.

3. Outline the pattern
lines with a V-tool.

Steps 4 - 6. Notice that as the tool moves through the cut, it stands up at the end to meet the stop cut.

Steps 7 - 9. Repeat
the preceding
approach.

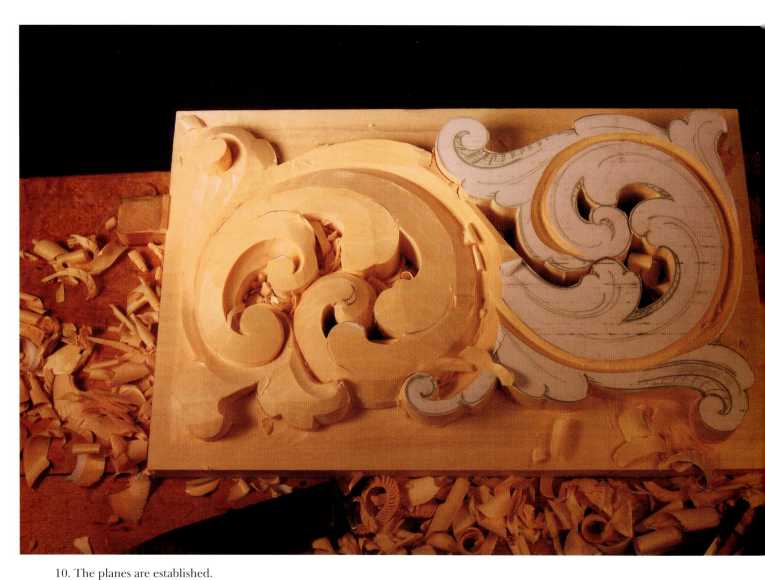

10. The planes are established.

Steps 11 & 12. Continue outlining the rest of the carving, remembering the grain.

Steps 13 - 16. The tool slides along and stands up at the end
of the cut to meet the stop cut which defines a leaf unfolding.

Steps 17 & 18. Establish the planes. Notice that the tool can be used turned over. See Chapter 4 for sharpening details.

Step 19. The entire carving is roughed out, ready for final clean up, back carving, and veining.

Step 20. The entire carving is completed.

Chapter 8
Finishing

Bring Out the Beauty of the Carving

You've worked hard on your acanthus carving; now on to the final step, the finishing. An entire book, *Finishing Techniques for Carvings*, is forthcoming. Until that time some of the more popular techniques will be generally explored in this section.

The most often asked question is, "Do I sand my carving?" The answer is no. With very sharp chisels, it is possible to obtain a mirror finish on the wood. At best, sandpaper will leave a surface similar in feel to suede. Creating a polished surface with sharp chisels is akin to a cabinetmaker scraping the surface of the wood rather than sanding to get a shine prior to applying any finish. Use your *chisels* to create a smooth surface. Whatever finishing technique you choose will accentuate the subtle planes your chisels have created.

8.1. Comparing Color Finishes

If you are going to leave the piece "natural," then use an oil based or acrylic varnish, a wax finish, clear shellac, a polyurethane or other commercially available clear finishes that may be mixtures of these. If you want to showcase the wood grain while still coloring the wood, try dyes, colored waxes, or thinned-out acrylic or artist's tube oils applied in transparent glazes for an "antique" look. Keep in mind that once you wax a piece, it is nearly impossible to apply a painted finish at a later date. Acrylic paints offer an easy way to finish pieces. While blending and creating depth can be tricky because these paints dry very quickly, they do offer a nice way to add color to your carving.

Slower-drying artist's tube oils offer the opportunity to blend colors wet-into-wet, creating a look that is unmatched by any other technique. Metal leaf or bronzing powders are two other options; they will accent each bevel and nuance of your carving (Figure 8.1). Leafing is a more difficult process to master, but can really make a carving sing. See Chapter 9, The Photo Gallery, for numerous examples. You may want to experiment with several finishing methods on scrap pieces of wood to see which will make the most of your carving before you actually work on your piece. Keep notes on the back of each piece so that you can replicate the effect later on.

Figure 8.1. Finish with bronzing powders.

Figure 8.2a.
Illustration of stain
with clear coat

Figure 8.2 b. Multicolor
oil finish

8.2. Sealing or Clear Coats

Regardless of the final look you choose, whether left in natural wood, stained, painted or metal leafed, it is necessary to seal the wood prior to continuing. This is typically accomplished by using a coat of sanding sealer, clear shellac, lacquer or a pre-stain treatment available at paint stores. Follow the manufacturer's instructions, and remember to take into account your final goals. For example, a thick coat of shellac will cause subsequent water-based materials to bead up. If you are using a stain, a pre-stain treatment will help the different wood grain exposed to absorb the stain more evenly. A thin coat of your chosen sealer should be sufficient (Figure 8.2a).

8.3. Priming Your Piece

If you plan to paint or leaf your piece, priming the wood is advisable. Use an acrylic primer for acrylics, and oil-based flat primer for an oil paint finish. Note that if you are going to use transparent glazes, you should not prime your piece. To prime, apply two subsequent thin coats of primer, letting each dry according to manufacturer's instructions. This may raise the grain, and so must be carefully sanded. Take care not to sand down through the primer, and into your piece. 220 grit sandpaper is usually gentle enough; some people prefer 0000 steel wool, or synthetic steel wool, which doesn't leave steel fibers on your piece. A third, and sometimes fourth coat of primer is necessary to obtain a glass-like undercoat, ready for a topcoat of color or leaf. When applying any paint, use a soft bristle brush that will leave as few brushstrokes as possible. You want the viewer of your artwork to see the carving and not the brushstrokes (Figure 8.2b).

8.4. Metallic Finishes

You may choose to paint most of your piece, and then use metal leaf or bronzing powders to accent certain areas. Gilding, or the application of metal leaf, is a delicate process, and will be covered in great detail in a future book, *Finishing Techniques for Carvings*. Practicing on another object before you attempt to leaf your carving is always advisable.

Metal leaf is available in different karats of yellow gold, white gold, silver, palladium, aluminum, and Dutch metal, which looks similar to gold but tarnishes. Variegated leaf is leaf with a multitude of colors on each piece. Silver leaf tarnishes very easily, and so is usually used only for glass gilding. On wood carvings white gold, aluminum leaf or palladium is preferred. Metal leaf is applied to the surface by using a special brush, called a gilder's tip, to gently place it on a glue-like varnish called "size." Let the size dry enough to get sticky or tack up. The open time is the amount of time you have to leaf before the size completely dries. When leafing, it is difficult to completely cover the entire area, so often the final undercoat is tinted according to what the leaf color will be. A yellow undercoat would be used for gold and Dutch metal (imitation gold) and a gray undercoat for white gold, aluminum, and palladium. For an antique effect, deep red can be used as an undercoat for gold or Dutch metal. Then if there are any "holidays", or areas that were missed with the size, or areas where the leaf refuses to stick, they will be much less pronounced than if the undercoat was white. Leaf is very fragile, and you may want to top coat it with a clear gloss varnish when you are done.

Bronzing powders are metallic looking powders, either made of finely ground metal, colored mica or synthetic materials. These powders can be mixed with a clear medium, such as varnish, or dusted onto the size. When working with any type of powder, be certain to wear an appropriate dust mask and heed the manufacturers' warnings. The ground brass bronzing powders tend to tarnish, whereas the mica powders and synthetics are nonreactive. The micas come in a wild array of colors, and some have an iridescent sheen to them. They can be glazed over paint for special effects. Again, experiment first on something other than your finished piece to determine the look that you desire.

The finishing can greatly enhance your carving, but remember that the carving is the most important aspect of the piece. Let the viewer's eye play with the subtle curves and angles your chisels have left, and not be distracted by the finish. Refer to Chapter 9, The Photo Gallery, to view examples of carvings finished with acrylics, oils, wax, leaf, and bronzing powders.

Chapter 9
Photo Gallery

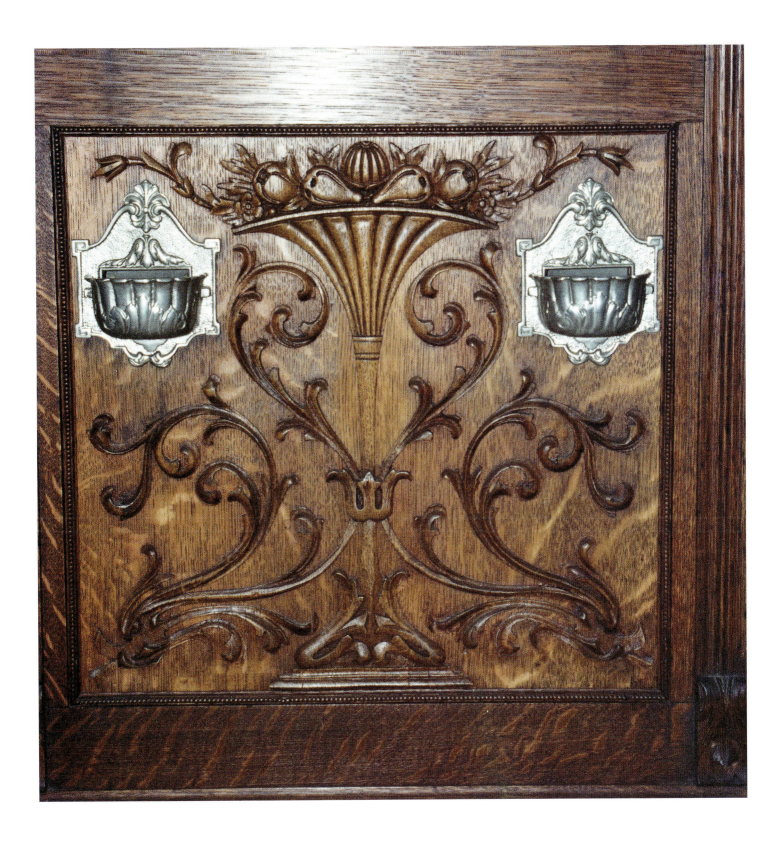

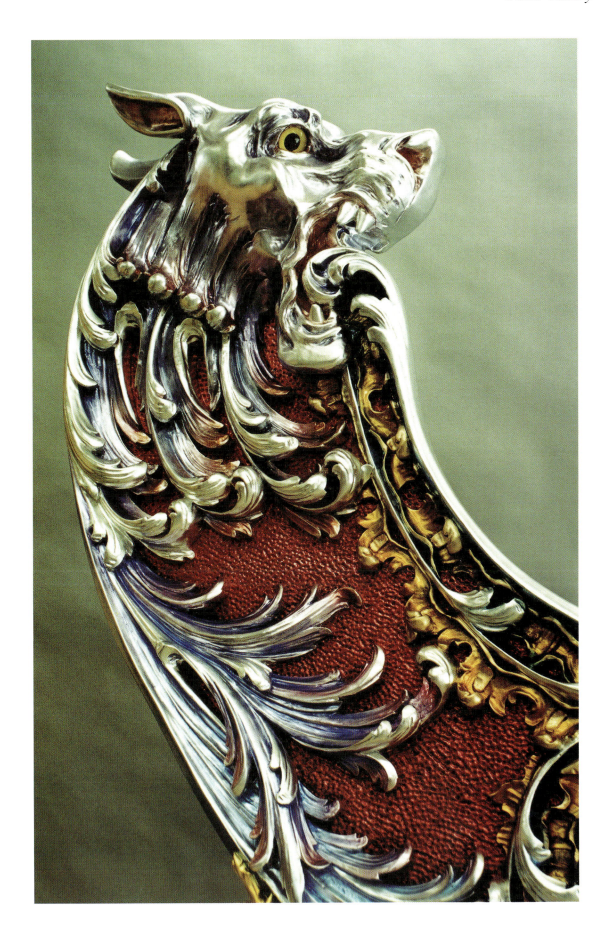

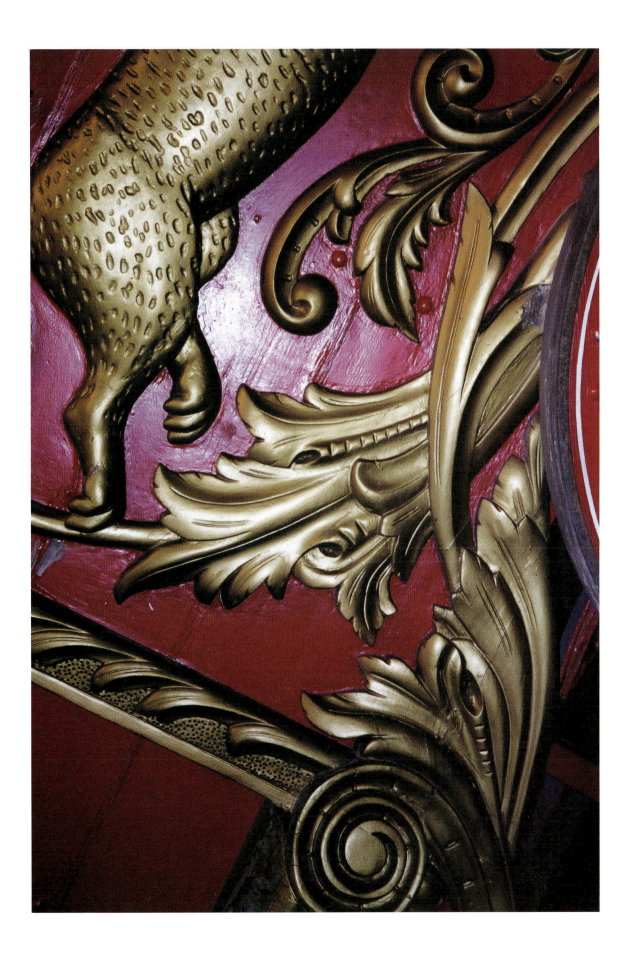

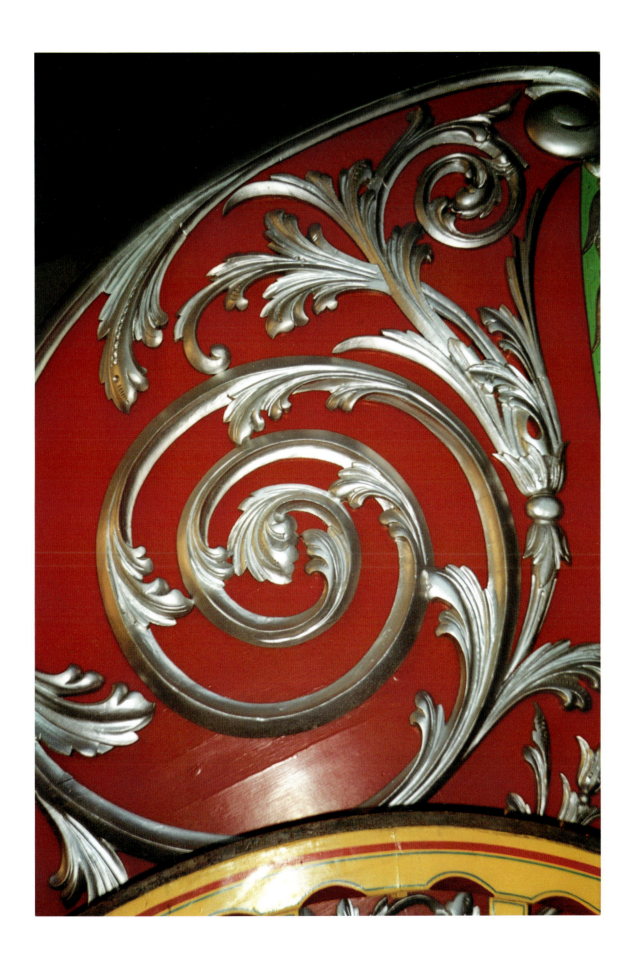

Chapter 10
Conclusion

In this book, the elements of acanthus design have been presented. With practice, drawing acanthus motifs will become easier and clearer. Notice examples of the design around you. Acanthus leaves are more prevalent than you think. As you gain more appreciation for the design, carving the flowing leaves will become much more understandable and therefore more readily accomplished.

Remember, when carving acanthus designs, whether on furniture, frames, signs or architectural elements, you must have extremely sharp tools. Any areas where the wood is tearing because the tool is not honed properly will jump out at the viewer. It is most definitely worth the effort to spend some time practicing sharpening and honing your tools. The rewards will be immense.

Elements of acanthus motifs will enhance almost any project and heretofore there has been no single source that summarizes the approach, design, and creation of this most beautiful feature.

If you would like further information, patterns, study models, supplies or class schedules, please see: **www.acanthuscarving.com**.

We sincerely hope that you enjoy the process of creating and carving acanthus enhanced projects.

Glossary of Terms

Acanthus: Plant with flowers native to the Mediterranean & warmer parts of Asia & Africa.

Accelerated curve: A curve that gets progressively tighter.

Back carving: Carving on the reverse side of the carving to lighten the scrolls, leaves, and to create shadow.

Baroque: A style that features continuous scrolls and leaf forms.

Bas-relief: Pronounced "bah relief." The design protrudes slightly from the background with no undercuts.

Bear's breech: Common name for acanthus.

Bench: A workbench or carving table.

Bevel: The angle on the underside of the tip of the tool.

Bowed board: A board that arches up like a bow and arrow.

Corinthian column: A column with leaves at the top.

Crescent moons: The shape representing folds along the ridge of leaves and scrolls that cross over each other.

Crown: The top of the carving, often resembling a crown (of leaves). Usually tilting down toward the viewer.

Cupped board: A board that is "U" shaped along its length.

Donut rule: This is a reminder that grain direction changes four times on the inside and on the outside of a circle.

Dutch metal: Imitation gold leaf (that tarnishes).

Eye: The tip of the leaf that has not unfolded yet.

Ferrule: A metal tube on the tool handle that keeps it from cracking

Geiss fuss: Pronounced "gise foos," German for goat's foot. Goat's hoof marks resemble the veins in acanthus leaves.

Gilders tip: A wide, flat brush used to pick up leaf.

Heel: The bottom of the bevel on the underside of the tool.

Holidays: Voids where the metal leaf did not adhere to the sizing.

Hone (Honing): To polish the edge of a tool to a razor sharp finish.

Hooked board: A flat board where the end "hooks" to one side.

Jointer: A machine that planes one edge of a board to establish a straight reference edge.

Micro bevel: The tiny bevel on the inside of the blade that allows the tool to be used upside down.

Negative rake: The top of the cutting edge is raked back and the bottom of the tool leads, cutting first.

Open time: The amount of time that size remains tacky enough to apply leaf before it dries completely.

Outlining: Removing wood from the outside of a carving, so that wood will fall away from the pattern and not push into it.

Parting tool: Another name for V-tool.

Pierced panel: A panel where the wood between scrolls and leaves has been removed.

Planer: A machine that reduces the thickness of a board.

Root: The portion of the acanthus carving from which all other elements emanate, generally scroll-shaped.

Rococo: An ornamental style featuring scrolls and shells that is adjacent rather than continuous.

Roughing out: Creating a general rough overall shape prior to refining the carving.

Router: A hand held tool that spins very fast with cutters that establish profiles or remove wood quickly.

Sheffield numbers: numbers representing the shape of the tool and the sweep or curvature of the tool.

Size: A clear, glue-like varnish that adheres leaf to a substrate.

Skew chisel: A flat chisel that has an angled bevel on the end.

Spalted wood: Wood that has turned blue and brown due to being attacked by fungus.

Stop cut: A vertical cut pressed down into the carving so that the horizontal cut does not lift out a needed element.

Tack up: When size used for applying leaf dries and becomes just sticky enough to adhere leaf.

Tang: The base of the tool inside the handle, not seen.

Twisted board: A board that is twisted in a spiral fashion from end to end. It will not sit flat on a table.

Undercut: After the carving is completed, material is removed from the underside of the elements to add shadow.

V-tool: a "V" shaped tool used to outline and detail.

Variegated leaf: Multicolored leaf.

Veiner: A #11, U-shaped tool.

Veining: Applying lines to leaves to add detail and help establish flow (*see geiss fuss*). Some carvers use V-tools/parting tools, others use Veiners #11 or U-shaped tools.

Vertical grain: When viewing a board from its end, the grain is perpendicular to the face.

Tool Shape & Sheffield Numbers

SHEFFIELD TOOL NUMBERING SYSTEM

Tools vary in three main ways: Length (shorter for hobbyist and longer for professionals), straight and bent (long bent or short bent/spoon gouge). Straight chisels may also be flared at the end called fish tails. The width of the blade is usually indicated in millimeters (some companies use inches).

The numbers on the tool gives the sweep. A #1 is a flat chisel ground on both sides and a #2 is a skew (flat chisel with the edge ground on both sides at an angle). From #3 to #9 you have the gouges running from slightly curved to tightly curved. The #10 & 11 are U-shaped, #10 is a fluter and #11 is a veiner (deeper U). You have front bent (see description above: long and short bent), back bent tools (with the bevel ground on the top surface) and fish tails (where the end of the tool is flared). Each type of tool has it's own series of numbers in the Sheffield system indicating the style and the amount of curve. Additionally, after the type of tool is indicated, the width is given as well. Spoon shaped gouges are useful for doing background carving. V-tools or parting tools are described below.

Although the Sheffield numbering system is the most popular, different manufacturers might "interpret" the system differently. Therefore, a #5 made by one manufacturer might resemble a #6 from another. Some tool manufacturers may have their own unique numbering system (for example, Swiss Made/Pfeil has a #2 that is slightly off of flat and not a skew). You must always be careful in selecting tools and be certain that you are ordering what you want.

Sheffield Numbering system for tools:

Straight	Long Bent	Short Bent	Back Bent
1		21	
2		22	
2		23	
3	12	24	33
4	13	25	34
5	14	26	35
6	15	27	36
7	16	28	37
8	17	29	38
9	18	30	
10	19	31	
11	20	32	
39	40	43 **V-tools with 75° angle**	
41	42	44 **V-tools with 60° angle**	
45	46	**V-tools with 100° angle**	

Straight tools: The numbers #39, #41 and #45. These are V-shaped/parting tools. The #39 is a straight V-tool with a 75 degree angle, #41 has a 60 degree angle. The #45 has a 100 degree angle. Please note that some companies numbers may vary, so carefully study the numbers and illustrations of the manufacturer from whom you are ordering.

Long bent tools: The #40 is a long bent 75 degree V, #42 has a 60 degree V and #46 is a 100 degree V.

Short bent tools/spoon: The #43 is a 75 degree V tool and #44 is a 60 degree V.

Spoon bent skews: are indicated by #22 right hand skew and #23 left hand skew.

Fish tail tools: Indicated by form #48 followed by the sweep number or curvature of the tool and the width.

Bibliography

Brande, William Thomas & George William Cox. *A Dictionary of Science and Art Volume III*. Published 1867.

Page, James. *Guide for Drawing the Acanthus and Every Description of Ornamental Foliage*. Reprinted 1886.

http://ancienthistory.about.com/od/greekarthistory/g/acanthus.htm (August 8, 2009).

Resources

Acanthuscarving.com: A web site devoted to spreading information and materials about carving in the acanthus style. Supplies, books, patterns, study models and classes are available.

Institute of Classical Architecture & Classical America: www.classicist.org

Rockler: www.rockler.com
Vesterheim Museum: www.vesterheim.org
Woodcarvers Supply: www.woodcarverssupply.com
Woodcraft: www.woodcraft.com

Index